The
Meaningful
Manager

The
MEANINGFUL
MANAGER

How to Manage What Matters

JEFF SMITH, PhD

LIONCREST
PUBLISHING

THE MEANINGFUL MANAGER
How to Manage What Matters

ISBN   978-1-5445-2945-5   *Hardcover*

978-1-5445-2946-2   *Paperback*

978-1-5445-2947-9   *Ebook*

Contents

For Megs, Brooklyn, Symon, and Nolita,
who continue to teach me so much about meaning.

INTRODUCTION

Congratulations! You are a manager or are about to become a manager. You have an exceptional opportunity to advance your own career and impact both your people and your organization—positively or negatively.

Some people get into management because they are passionate about helping others. Others think it will help prepare them for a future leadership role or that they have to become a manager to advance their career. No matter why you became a manager, I am here to guide you. You can create value for your organization, find fulfillment and meaning in your role, and enjoy the ups and downs that come with managing people by becoming a meaningful manager.

You are probably overwhelmed by the number of leadership and management resources. I know I was. There are hundreds of thousands of books, videos, courses, and podcast episodes. This feeling of overwhelm is what led me to write another book on management.

So, what makes this book different?

It's fluff-free. Many business books contain five pages of valuable content within 250 pages. This book is already condensed to save you hours of time.

It's immediately actionable. For every idea or practice I introduce in this book, I include a simple guide or framework to help you to use it right away. I hope this book can be a reference that you come back to over and over again.

It's a complete operating system for managing other people. I reference and recommend dozens of other resources, but if you only use the practices in this book, you will be a great—if not excellent—manager who meaningfully impacts their people's work and lives. The other resources are optional.

Now seems like the right time to warn you that there's a multi-billion-dollar learning and development industry out there, full of gurus and thought leaders who create content and marketing aimed at making you feel incomplete. They want you to think you can't be successful unless you buy another product or service. I've been where you are—reading book after book, watching video after video, and listening to podcast after podcast.

Here's one of my favorite quotes, from Sophia Bush: "You are allowed to be both a masterpiece and a work in progress simultaneously."

I'm here to remind you that you are both a masterpiece and a work in progress.

This means that you can:

- Make a meaningful impact *right now*.

- Help your people increase their performance and fulfillment.

- Take control of your own career, no matter where you are in the organization.

- Take your impact and influence to another level.

You can become a meaningful manager *right now* by managing what matters. Yes, lifelong learning can be extremely enjoyable. It certainly is for me. But you can make a positive impact on yourself, your people, and your organization right now.

Get the most out of this book by taking notes and applying what you learn as you learn it. Let's get started.

PART 1

MEANINGFUL MANAGEMENT STARTS WITH YOU

Are you a meaningful manager or a mediocre manager?

The mediocre manager is unfocused and consistently over-whelmed. The meaningful manager increases performance, security, and growth by managing what matters.

The mediocre manager thinks you have to choose between people and performance. The meaningful manager knows you can choose both.

The mediocre manager is too busy for self-care and self-aware-ness. The meaningful manager knows that higher performance, security, and growth start with them.

The mediocre manager has unclear expectations for themself and their team. The meaningful manager cocreates clear, prioritized goals and agreements so people know where to focus their precious time and energy.

The mediocre manager thinks praise and encouragement are for the weak. The meaningful manager knows that making meaningful progress on meaningful work—and being regularly recognized for it—is essential for sustaining motivation and high performance.

The mediocre manager is scared to criticize their team because they want to be liked. The meaningful manager knows that people want to do well and that feedback fuels the higher performance they desire.

The mediocre manager only talks about what they need from their people. The meaningful manager appropriately balances their own needs, their people's needs, and their organization's needs.

The mediocre manager thinks they are protecting their people by hiding problems from them. The meaningful manager proactively involves their people in discovering and solving problems because overcoming challenges together increases performance, security, and growth.

The mediocre manager frequently cancels one-on-ones and complains about not having enough time to coach their people. The meaningful manager prioritizes frequent, empowering conversations with their people, focused on helping them achieve and grow.

The mediocre manager is afraid to get personal because it might be uncomfortable. The meaningful manager honors each individual's needs, seeing and supporting their people, especially when it's hard.

The mediocre manager assumes that if no one is complaining, everything is okay. The meaningful manager proactively requests feedback from their team about what's going well and what can be improved.

The mediocre manager thinks they know what's best. The meaningful manager helps their team understand goals and challenges to make better decisions together.

The mediocre manager believes they have to have all the answers. The meaningful manager isn't afraid to say, "I don't know."

The mediocre manager avoids conflict. The meaningful manager is compassionate and direct, even when there's discomfort, and requires the same from their whole team.

The mediocre manager has a disorganized approach to managing their people. The meaningful manager has a simple system for managing what matters.

The mediocre manager thinks they've seen it all before. The meaningful manager never stops learning, realizing they are a masterpiece and a work in progress, just like everyone on their team.

The mediocre manager helps their people succeed at work. The meaningful manager helps their people succeed at work and connect to their larger purpose, contributing to success, well-being, and fulfillment at work and beyond.

This book is your guide for becoming a meaningful manager.

CHAPTER 1

FOCUSING ON
SELF-AWARENESS

You have daily opportunities to significantly impact others around you. To maximize your impact and fulfillment, start with self-awareness.

Self-awareness is a lifelong endeavor. We all learn, grow, adapt, and evolve throughout our entire lives. We believe we know ourselves, but then an experience reveals a hidden strength, blind spot, or opportunity for growth and dramatically changes our values.

Importantly, remember that you can be successful by being yourself. Don't feel like you have to embody antiquated leadership stereotypes such as extraordinary extroversion or a win-at-any-cost attitude. Anyone can be a successful manager and leader. There's no type or set of strengths that's required. Be your best self, not an imitation of someone else.

We are going to simplify our approach to self-awareness by focusing on meaning, passions, strengths, values, and vision. Revisit these topics at least every six months to help you understand how you are learning, growing, and transforming.

MEANING

Meaning is about understanding your purpose, sometimes called your "why." Meaning involves the important things you want to fulfill in your life. Meaning provides a clear sense of direction. Meaning makes the time, energy, and effort you put into your work and life feel worthwhile. Your purpose can appear early in life—for example, someone who has wanted to be a designer since they were a child. Your purpose can also reveal itself later or after a change in perspective or circumstance—for example, a teacher who realizes they want to be a nurse after caring for an ailing loved one.

Meaning also includes the belief that you are significant and valuable. Because meaning often involves feeling connected to something greater than yourself, meaning and purpose are often about positively impacting others and the world around you. However, I want to remind you that while other people and causes matter, so do you. You have to invest in your own health, well-being, and self-care to reach your highest potential and maximize the positive impact you have on others.

As you are thinking about meaning, ask yourself these questions:

- When does expending your energy feel most worthwhile?

- What do you want to be known for?

- How do you want to be remembered?

- What do you feel called to do?

- What do you want someone to say during your eulogy?

- How does your purpose transcend money?

- What's your why? Why do you do the activities you do? Why do you make the decisions you make?

In summary, what fulfills and inspires you? From a professional point of view, I feel fulfilled and inspired when I help leaders and organizations both love their people and achieve their organization's mission.

If you are struggling to find your purpose, reflect on your passions and interests, things that you are curious about, activities that you enjoy, and experiences that energize you. Importantly, remember that you and your purpose may evolve and change. Sometimes, people feel too much pressure to discover their life's purpose instead of focusing on their current purpose. You can have a number of purposes throughout your life. You can also find meaning in multiple endeavors at the same time. For example, someone may find meaning in managing a product team at work and loving their partner and dogs in life.

These are deep questions. Please take a moment to reflect on your responses.

PASSIONS

Passions are strong inclinations toward self-defining activities that you like. Passion can be so intense that you might say you love the activity. Passions can be harmonious, balancing your needs with the needs of others. Passions can also be obsessive, leading to burnout and other challenges. Your passions may change and evolve over time.

As you are considering your passions, ask yourself these questions:

- Where are you willing and eager to put in energy and effort?

- Where do you find yourself completely absorbed in your work or other activities?

- What sparks your curiosity?

- What piques your interest?

- What naturally energizes you?

Marketing is an example of a current passion of mine. I could review ads, brainstorm about campaigns, read about the latest trends, and listen to podcasts about marketing for hours. What energizes you?

If you are having trouble thinking of any activities that energize you, consider talking to a mental health professional. I speak with a cognitive-behavioral therapist weekly, and she is invaluable for my health and well-being. If you aren't sure what you are passionate about, keep trying new activities, and fake it until you make it!

STRENGTHS

Strengths describe what you naturally do best. I'll try to avoid making too many concepts "my favorite" throughout this book, but strengths are definitely one of them. Aligning one's prioritized goals, role, and strengths can increase productivity, impact, fulfillment, and even joy, so it's important to know your strengths and use them on a consistent basis.

Some people are natural strategists, while others are natural executors. Some people can inspire an entire room, while others specialize in deep, personal connections. Any combination of strengths can be the foundation of successful management and leadership. Strengths include courage, creativity, and compassion for others.

My favorite three strengths assessments are Gallup's Clif-tonStrengths™, Tilt 365's True Tilt Profile, and VIA's Survey of Character Strengths. Each of the assessments is worth the investment in money and time. Using these assessments can accelerate not only your self-awareness but also how well you understand your team. Strongly consider using these assessments for yourself, your team, and your organization.

If you do invest in a strengths assessment, remember that your strengths are a foundation for your achievements, security, and growth. Awareness of your strengths should elevate your self-confidence and sense of possibility, but some strengths assessments make it seem like you can only learn and grow in an area of strength. This is a fundamental mistake. You, your strengths, and your skills are not fixed. Growth may be more challenging in some areas than others, but people can learn and grow in nearly infinite ways.

Here are a few questions to ask yourself to help determine your strengths:

- What brings you the most satisfaction?

- What activities do you most enjoy?

- When does success feel easier?

- When do learning and growth feel most natural?

- When do you feel powerful?

You can also ask others what they think your strengths are. Simply say, "I'm reading a book about how to become a better manager and leader. It says to ask others what I do best, and I value your opinion. What do you think I do best?" If you like, you can share what you think the other person does best as part of your response.

Combine results from different assessments with your own reflections and observations from others. Look for themes, and compare them to your own experiences. Does using these strengths feel natural, easier, and empowering?

Boldness is a strength that shows up for me across various assessments. I have a bias for action and often think the best way to decide on a course of action is to act and learn along the way. I need to be mindful about taking boldness too far and becoming reckless.

Once you understand your strengths, apply them at work and in life. Look for ways to use your strengths to accomplish your vision and goals. Many people are surprised to hear they should use their strengths in life, not just at work. If you only use your strengths at work, you are missing opportunities to positively influence other areas of your life.

Ask yourself:

- How often are you using one or more of your strengths at work and beyond?

- How often do you feel instinctual and successful?

- How often do your accomplishments and growth happen naturally and even easily?

Often, our greatest weaknesses are overused strengths. A lack of courage is cowardice. Too much courage is recklessness. A lack of compassion for others is callousness. Too much compassion for others can lead to martyrdom and a lack of healthy selfishness. Watch out for overused strengths, especially when you're under a lot of stress.

VALUES

Values describe what is most important to you.

At the organizational level, your values will inform how you hire and fire people based on your values. Note that hiring for values fit does not mean hiring the same exact people. Hire people who add to your culture. As an individual, your values should reflect what's most important to you at this moment in time. Here are some examples to help you get started:

- Accomplishment

- Adventure

- Community

- Compassion

- Equity

- Family

- Friendship

- Freedom

- Fitness

- Fun

- Growth

- Independence

- Learning

- Money/Financial Security

- Peak Experiences

- Power

- Relationships

- Safety

- Self-Care

- Spirituality

- Status

- Well-Being

Remember that your values may change or evolve over time. For example, traveling used to be a top value for me because I enjoyed experiencing new places. I am now nourishing my value of adventure through deeper interactions with nature, such as hiking and camping. At the beginning of my career, my value of impact was nourished primarily by my business impact; now it's about business outcomes as well as societal and human outcomes.

Consider starting with three to five values. Again, these most likely won't be permanent, so don't worry about perfection. I like using a "title: subtitle" framework to document values. This means a one- or two-word value with a three-to-seven-word description. Here are my values as I write this, for example:

- Honesty: Tell the truth with compassion.

- Love: Listen and act with compassion and empathy.

- Impact: Create positive change.

- Exploration: Fortune favors the bold.

- Growth: Always be learning.

Take a few moments to write down your values and what's most important to you. Now, ask yourself:

- How much do your values align with how you are spending your time?

- How much do your values align with how you are spending your energy? Are you using your best energy on what matters most to you?

- How often are you prioritizing those fundamentally nonnegotiable, most critical things for you?

Periodically review how you are spending your time and energy to help you reflect, regroup, and reprioritize. I attempt to do this once per month. If you are like me and many other people, you'll find that you are not always spending your time and energy on your values. Some months, I invest my time and energy in alignment with my values, which helps me feel energized and impactful. But other months, when I'm less aligned, I often feel unproductive, frustrated, and unfulfilled. Schedule a monthly meeting with yourself to review your values and how well you are living them.

VISION

Your vision is a clear map for growth, with milestones and destinations. This vision should reflect who you are and who you want to become as a whole person. Your vision combines meaning, passions, strengths, and values and represents the life you want at work and beyond. It influences the decisions you make, how you spend your time and money, and who you connect with and disconnect from.

Visions are often unclear. Let's say I told you to imagine a house with two bedrooms. How many different variations of houses with two bedrooms are there? It could be anything from an urban apartment to a cabin in the woods. What if I said to imagine a vehicle with four doors? It could be a rally car, station wagon, or extended-cab truck.

Your vision should be clear enough that you can easily imagine it—and even feel it! Use all your senses—sight, hearing, smell, taste, and touch—to ensure your vision is clear enough to inspire you and help you make the right decisions. Use your sense of intuition and insight that extends beyond the traditional five senses as well.

A three-year vision provides enough time for possibility without adding the fog of too far in the future. Aim for your vision to be around five hundred words, so it has the right amount of actionable clarity and detail. Dare to dream big during this exercise, and don't worry about execution as much right now. For the moment, pretend that this will happen. Focus on the growth and transformation you want to create in your life.

Here are a few questions to reflect on as you create your vision:

- What's most important to you?

- What will you accomplish?

- What would success mean?

- How do you feel on a day-to-day basis?

- How do you feel about yourself?

- Who are you partnering with?

- What is your personal brand?

- What are you known for?

- What does your average day look and feel like?

- What does your average week look and feel like?

- Who are you learning from?

- What have you learned?

- What new skills have you acquired?

- Who is a positive influence on your life?

- Who do you positively influence? How do you influence them?

When creating your vision, remember to focus on meaning, passions, values, and strengths. Describe your whole self and whole life at work and beyond. It's okay if work gives you meaning—or doesn't. Work can be a means to meaning elsewhere.

Also remember to be selfish in a healthy way. This is about what you want and need, not about obligation to someone else. This is your vision for you, not someone else's vision for you. You matter. You are worth the investment.

Don't forget to challenge traditional rules and boundaries. Remember that you are a masterpiece and a work in progress, capable of tremendous possibility.

I recommend starting with a list of what's most important to you and your responses to the questions above. Give yourself permission to create a draft or a few drafts, and then add details later after some reflection. Then turn your list and responses into a descriptive, invigorating story about yourself. Finally, create a ceremony where you review and consult it regularly—at least once per month. For example, schedule a monthly one-hour meeting with yourself to review your vision and values. If three years seems like too much, create a vision for the next ninety days. After those ninety days, create your three-year vision.

Your vision guides you as you guide your people. I recommend guiding your people through this process as well. However, don't involve yourself too much. Allow them to create their vision on their own without too much influence from you. Coach and guide them if they decide to ask you questions or share their vision with you. Your presence in the process may influence them in ways that neither of you are aware of.

DISCOVERING OR REDISCOVERING THE VALUE, JOY, AND FULFILLMENT OF MEANINGFUL MANAGEMENT

You can substantially influence the quality of your team members' work. You can also significantly influence the quality of their lives. You can inspire, motivate, and encourage. You can help your people feel seen and valued. You can transform meaningless work into meaningful work. You can support your people as they discover themselves, their values, and their value. You can help them develop not only as employees but as humans.

Unfortunately, in many organizations, management and even leadership feel more obligatory than inspirational. Often, people take management roles because that's the only way to get promoted, but managers and leaders aren't always trained well or given the tools and technology they need.

Fortunately, you have control of how you manage and lead your people. Even if you work at a lackluster organization, you can create a compelling workplace for your people anyway. You can uplift and strengthen them. You can take your own career to the next level by helping the people on your team.

Here are a few ways that meaningful management can be fulfilling for you and your people:

- Meaning: creating a positive impact that matters

- Relationships: developing connections with others

- Community: uniting with others around a common vision, unmet need, or shared value

- Achievement: accomplishing what you set out to do

- Growth: learning new knowledge and skills

- Self-actualization: realizing and even increasing your highest potential

As a manager and leader, you can choose to be a supervisor who just approves vacation and completes performance reviews, or you can inspire, motivate, and help people feel energized and fulfilled. Since you're reading this, I am excited and encouraged that you are choosing the latter.

CHAPTER 2

THE THREE THINGS THAT MATTER

Successful management starts with prioritizing what you, your people, and your organization want to accomplish. Without proper prioritization, people may focus on the wrong things. Focusing on the wrong things wastes time, money, and energy. Focusing on the right things can lead to the greatest performance improvements. Productivity hacks that increase productivity by a few percentage points are helpful, but they are nothing compared to increasing the time that someone invests in what matters most from 50 percent to 90 percent.

There are three things that matter most: performance, security, and growth.

PERFORMANCE

Performance is about organizational performance, team performance, and individual performance.

Organizational and Team Performance

An organization's performance includes financial performance, ethical performance, and purposeful performance. People and teams that significantly impact organizational performance are valuable, so look for ways to positively impact your organization's performance. Aligning your team's performance to your organization's performance helps your people understand why they invest their time, talent, and energy into their work for thousands of hours every year.

You will be held accountable for the accomplishments and shortcomings of your team. In most organizations, one person can accomplish very little on their own, so team performance is critical. Even superstar engineers and salespeople need support, information, and more from others. Many managers and leaders underestimate the influence they can have on their team's performance and culture. You can create a fantastic team culture even in a lackluster organization. You may have to start smaller, but you can make a significant difference with or without organizational support.

Financial Performance

The most important metrics that reflect an organization's financial performance vary. A startup might be focused on high growth at an acceptable burn rate. A larger organization might be focused on a financial metric like return on invested capital (ROIC). I have never worked at a company that didn't care deeply about revenue, margins, profit or potential future profit (sometimes including unit economics), growth, churn (the loss of customers), retention (sometimes expressed as dollar-based net retention rate or DBNRR, pronounced "dub-ner"), and expansion (customer growth after the initial purchase). Understand these basic terms, and find ways to impact them.

The reality is that your own executives, your board, and the market speak the language of business, so you and your people need to as well. Understand the ways that your work influences your organization's financial performance. To learn more from an approachable resource, I recommend the book *Financial Intelligence* and the website and book *The Personal MBA*.

Don't be afraid to ask simple, hard questions to help you and your people decide how to invest your time. For example, which is more important for our organization right now: new customers, customer retention, or profitability? Are we focused on adding new features, reducing technical debt, or optimizing existing features? The initial answer might be that all three are important, but understanding their relative importance is critical for you and your team.

Clearly align your team's work to your organization's financial performance. Everyone on your team should understand why their work matters to an organization's most important goals. If you can't make the connection yourself, partner with someone on your finance team. Financial performance shouldn't be considered a sales and marketing thing or a customer-facing thing. Product, design, and engineering teams create the things that your customers buy. Finance and HR teams help align people, processes, and resources against an organization's goals and opportunities. Leadership creates strategies that influence decision-making throughout your organization. Financial performance depends on everyone.

Ethical Performance

Ethical performance is about your organization's legal and ethical responsibilities. Beyond philosophical concerns about morality, ethical performance matters because legal and ethical breaches destroy relationships and organizations. Familiarize yourself with the legal and ethical considerations related to your work. This includes workplace laws, contractual obligations, and policies contained in critical documents like your employee handbook. Understand essential topics like hostile work environments, diversity, equity, inclusion, harassment, bullying, and fraud.

Depending on your organization, ethical performance may be included in your organization's values. For example, I worked at an exceptional company where one of our values was integrity. Integrity meant speaking the truth courageously. People throughout the organization were held accountable for integrity.

If you lose sight of how your organization accomplishes your objectives from an ethical and legal point of view, you are introducing extraordinary risk in your organization. If you find yourself in an ethical or legal situation where you aren't sure what to do, consult counsel. Ideally, your senior leadership team and counsel will identify, quantify, and mitigate risks in a proactive, ongoing way.

Ethical performance is also critical at the team level. You set the standard for how important your people think ethical, legal, and values-related considerations are. It's been said that what you permit, you promote. When you have a question, follow your processes and consult your counsel.

Purposeful Performance

Purposeful performance includes your vision, your mission, your triple bottom line, and your dent in the universe. Why does your organization exist? Why does your team exist?

People want more from work than ever: paycheck, purpose, perks, benefits, community, meaning, career opportunities, and fulfillment. This means that your organization's vision should be more than "be the market leader in X." It should also be about the change (however large or small) you want to bring to the world. People want to do meaningful work, and they want to be seen, heard, and noticed as they make meaningful progress on that work. It's your responsibility to show them and remind them why their work matters to your organization and your stakeholders. Have them meet their customers or stakeholders. Draw a visualization or simple sketch showing how their work positively impacts the world. Quantify the impact if possible. Always tell stories about how important your team's work is. Repeat and update these stories often.

If your organization hasn't made your purpose clear, use your influence to make your purpose clear and inspiring to your stakeholders, including your people, customers, prospects, partners, shareholders, investors, and analysts who cover your space.

In the meantime, create a meaningful purpose for your team. Rally your team around it. Cocreate a purpose with them, and gather qualitative feedback to ensure your purpose is meaningful to them. Make sure your people know why they matter and why their work matters. Ideally, your organization will report on metrics related to your purposeful performance. If it doesn't, ask your senior leadership team to start. Create a business case to justify reporting on your purposeful performance. Start with talent acquisition costs related to replacing the people on your team who are leaving for more meaningful work.

Individual Performance

Motivating and measuring the performance of individuals on your team are critical responsibilities. Performance management can quickly become complicated. A comprehensive, multifaceted approach seems like more work up front, but it actually saves you and your people time because they know exactly what's agreed upon.

I recommend understanding the following about each of your people:

Values

How well do they represent the values of your organization? Values should come from the organizational level. If your organization does not have clear values or you feel like something is missing, consider creating values that are specific to your team. For example, your organization's "innovation" value may not feel relevant to your customer support team, but you and your customer support team can be innovative. Innovation can happen anywhere in an organization.

Outcomes

What do you want them to accomplish? Did they accomplish it? Outcomes matter more than activity or availability. Give your people clear goals that reflect what you want them to accomplish. Focus on outcomes and provide as much flexibility as you can. Let people work when and where they want whenever possible.

Quantity

How much did they produce? Quantity should be related to the outcome, not the underlying activities.

Quality

Does their work meet your standards? For example, is their code testable and relatively bug-free? Are their customers staying with your organization or churning right away? Do customers thrive and grow under their care? Does someone need to double-check their work?

Complexity

How challenging is the work they are completing? Do they handle problems that other people can't solve? Are they the team's go-to person on a complex topic? Do they artificially inflate their quantity and quality numbers by focusing on simple problems?

Influence

How are they impacting others on their team and in your organization? Do they energize and uplift their teammates? Do they offer valuable ideas and information to other teams? Do they coach or mentor others?

Context

What's going on in the world, within your industry and market, and in their life? Context should always be considered during performance reviews. As I am writing this, a global pandemic has shaken up every economy and many industries. People are under an exceptional amount of stress, and many are isolated from human connection.

That said, considering context doesn't mean that you shouldn't review performance. People identify with their work. They want work that matters, and they want to be seen and recognized at work. Reviewing someone's work shows that they matter and their work matters. Don't miss out on the powerful impact of reviewing individual performance.

Effectively Measuring Performance

To measure performance, start with your values. Hire and fire people based on values and outcomes. Create goals focused on outcomes, and give people freedom to achieve those outcomes. If you don't measure how people complete their goals (i.e., your values), then people will focus on outcomes over values.

Measure and evaluate what people accomplish and how they accomplish it. If you don't measure quantity, quality, and complexity together, people will—either intentionally or unintentionally—find ways to "play the game" rather than perform. Balance your goals. Your people should always know how well or poorly they are performing based on clear goals and agreements.

Give feedback on performance frequently. Don't wait for an annual or quarterly performance review. Hold people accountable if they aren't successful. Help them understand how they might improve or try different approaches. If you don't hold people accountable, you are saying their work doesn't matter. This can create a vicious cycle where performance decreases because you are communicating that it doesn't make a difference whether they perform or not. Work with your people/HR team as you notice performance issues. People or HR can partner with you to substantially improve someone's performance or take appropriate action if you can't.

Encourage your people to challenge themselves. Achievement is part of thriving, so recognize and savor their successes, and help them grow from failure. Remember to hold people with higher compensation accountable to higher standards, even if they have the same role. Performance agreements may need to be adjusted for location depending on your organization's approach to compensation.

SECURITY

You're managing humans and need to understand their needs. I often use the phrase "whole-person needs" to remind us that people aren't cogs in a machine. They have dreams, fears, motivations, strengths, weaknesses, and lives outside of work. A valuable framework is Maslow's hierarchy of needs. In his book *Transcend: The New Science of Self-Actualization*, Scott Barry Kaufman aligned Maslow's work to scientific research using a sailboat model that describes how humans have security needs (the boat) and growth needs (the sail) to reach their highest potential. Meaningful managers deeply appreciate the relationship between security and growth.

Security creates a foundation for performance and growth. When security needs are met, your people are more likely to feel a sense of belonging, connection, and opportunity in your organization. When security needs are not met, your people will be worried, isolated, and frustrated. You can measure whether your team members' security needs are met through direct conversations, confidential means such as engagement surveys, and anonymous means such as software that hides who shared the feedback.

Part of managing what matters is keeping things simple, so we are going to reduce the list of dozens of security needs down to seven impactful needs:

Safety

Safety is about minimizing real and perceived physical, psychological, and financial risks, including uncertainty about the future of your organization or role, the presence of bullying or sexual harassment, or unsafe practices such as not wearing protective gear. Without a foundation of safety, it's challenging and sometimes impossible for someone to achieve their goals. Proactively monitor and look for threats to the safety of your people and team. Then take action and repeat the process.

Diversity, Equity, Inclusion, and Belonging

Diversity, equity, inclusion, and belonging are essential requirements for organizations. Diversity is the degree that organizations value differences. Diversity starts with your employer brand and recruiting and continues throughout your entire employee experience. Equity means striving toward fair opportunities and compensation for everyone. Equity requires objective data as well as benchmarking and other feedback loops from within your organization. Inclusion is treating people in a way that honors and satisfies individual needs for belonging.

Create a team that welcomes, honors, and appreciates differences. Encourage your team to connect deeply with others. Continuously involve your team in increasing diversity, equity, and inclusion by requesting feedback and perspectives on how to improve.

Diversity, equity, and inclusion are not side projects; they are essential for success. Hold yourself and your leadership accountable for diversity, equity, and inclusion initiatives and results.

Psychological Safety

Psychological safety is about feeling like you can take risks at work, bring up problems and tough issues, and reveal your unique talents and skills. Create ceremonies for surfacing what's going well and what can be improved. Start with your own opportunities for improvement. Retrospectives or debriefs every two weeks get your team involved in its own improvement and growth. Amy Edmondson's research emphasizes the importance of psychological safety for learning. Make it okay to make mistakes within reason, but unacceptable to hide them and not learn from them.

Meaningful Relationships

Meaningful relationships involve expressing your feelings to others, taking time to understand others, and investing in the development of meaningful connections. Foster meaningful relationships with each of your team members and between them through regular conversations, deep listening, and supporting them however you can.

Autonomy

Autonomy is about being free to do things your own way and express your authentic self. Clearly define what someone needs to accomplish, and provide latitude regarding how they accomplish it when possible. In addition, give your people freedom to pursue their own interests at work and beyond.

Strengths Discovery and Alignment

Strengths discovery involves understanding your strengths and your team's strengths, and strengths alignment means ensuring that your people are using their strengths to accomplish their goals. A simple question such as "How and how often are you using your strengths to accomplish your goals?" can reveal opportunities for improved productivity and fulfillment.

Self-Esteem

Self-esteem is about being comfortable with yourself and secure in your sense of self-worth. Help your people understand their strengths and recognize the tremendous power they possess. Many people focus too much on shortcomings, mistakes, and weaknesses rather than strengths and capabilities. Help them see themselves as masterpieces and works in progress.

GROWTH

The need for growth reflects our human desire to learn, explore, and find meaning at work and beyond. Your people want opportunities to grow, learn new skills, and conquer new challenges. It's also important to offer growth opportunities through promotions, compensation, and total rewards.

Needs related to growth include the following:

Purpose and Meaning

Purpose and meaning are about believing that you have something important to accomplish. Viktor Frankl's *Man's Search for Meaning* argues that our primary drive as humans is meaning. Your people need to know why their work matters to your organization, your organization's mission, and other people. Create experiences where your people meet the people they positively impact. This might mean inviting a customer or colleague to one of your meetings. I have found that teams who don't usually interact with customers cherish first-hand, personal stories about the impact your products and services have on other people. You can also take people to your customers. After seeing products in action, engineers can refer back to those experiences for months as they build and improve your products. Having the real people you impact in mind as you work motivates and inspires.

Mattering

Mattering is about feeling valued and making meaningful contributions. People want to be trusted and relied upon for support, and they need to know their work makes a real difference and contributes to something larger than themselves. Frequently remind your people how much you appreciate them.

Flow

Flow is full immersion, energized, focused, and deep enjoyment of an activity. Being in flow is sometimes referred to as being "in the zone" and often involves losing yourself in your work. It's hard, if not impossible, to experience flow when you are frequently interrupted, so ensure that your people have time for deep work, uninterrupted work.

A proper balance of challenge and skill is part of flow as well. Mihaly Csikszentmihalyi's groundbreaking research on flow also notes that while too much challenge can lead to anxiety, too little challenge can result in boredom. As manager, ensure that your people are challenged. Give people more responsibility than you might be comfortable with to see what they can do. A team lead early in my career asked me to lead a project involving a multimillion-dollar problem related to service technicians replacing parts that weren't actually defective. The project required months to understand our product's design, untangle our service and support processes, and meet with at least a hundred different stakeholders and customers. We ended up saving the organization a significant amount of money and highlighting additional opportunities for cost savings. After I completed the project, my team lead told me that he never thought I could do it in the time he gave me. I'm glad he didn't tell me that before I began!

Progress

Progress is about having clear short-term goals and regularly making meaningful headway. It also involves being seen and recognized for that progress. This can nourish motivation, as noted in Teresa Amabile's work on progress and small wins. Help your people break goals into smaller goals and projects, and recognize their effort and progress along the way. Recognition for wins and progress is one of the most impactful and cost-effective ways to motivate your people.

Peak Experiences

Peak experiences involve feelings of possibility, oneness, and transcendence. They often include the feeling of new horizons opening up for you. Peak experiences can promote selflessness, where you feel profoundly connected with others. Create peak experiences for your people at work and beyond to help them understand and appreciate themselves as humans, not just employees.

Self-Actualization

Self-actualization is about realizing one's potential and operating at one's full capacity. It's critical to note that people can increase their potential. Potential is not fixed. Remind your people to have a personal growth mindset as they aim to be and become all that they can be.

REMEMBERING THE THREE THINGS THAT MATTER

You may be thinking, *Wow! That's too much to remember.* Continuously focus on supporting your people with regard to performance, security, and growth. You don't need to remember every term on this list. You can always refer back to *The Meaningful Manager* as you go deeper and create new processes. In the meantime, here are a few simple (not easy) questions to help you and your people:

- Performance: Are your people achieving what you need from them in a way that lines up with your organizational goals, values, and purpose?

- Security: Do your people feel safe, included, and valued for who they are?

- Growth: Are your people making progress, developing their strengths, and reaching their highest potential?

The foundation and practices in the next chapter will help you keep performance, security, and growth top of mind.

Chapter 3

The Foundation of Managing What Matters

To manage what matters, start with what matters: performance, security, and growth. Then, create a foundation for the practices that will help you as you manage what matters. The foundation is presence, empathy, and agreements. Don't skip this chapter because you think these are soft skills. Few things will complicate your role as a manager and limit your career advancement more than a lack of these foundational elements. Without presence, your people will think they and their work don't matter to you. Without empathy, you won't connect with your people or be able to coach them effectively. Without agreements, you'll let your people down, and they won't trust you. If you want to be a manager people are motivated to work for and who can coach their people as a trusted, valued partner in their performance, security, and growth, let's begin.

PRESENCE

Presence involves being where you are, focusing your attention, and deeply perceiving your current activity. It's natural for you to be mentally distracted by an upcoming meeting, something going on outside of work, or even a daydream. Many people nod their heads and just try to make it through the day, but deeply perceiving involves an additional level of focus and curiosity.

Focusing your attention means doing one thing at a time. You can think of attention as a spotlight. When you attempt to do more than one thing at a time, you are swinging your spotlight back and forth between those things, which wastes your time and energy.

Schedule time for your own deep work so you aren't catching up on messages and other work during your one-on-ones and meetings. Make sure you include short breaks between meetings if you have to respond to messages rapidly.

You have an exceptional opportunity to make a meaningful impact on your people every day. For example, recognize effort and impact by asking questions and giving specific compliments. Go beyond just "good job" and describe the accomplishment and the impact it had.

When you are in a conversation or meeting with your people, be there fully by asking questions to understand challenging situations, taking notes, and contributing to the conversation without giving advice. Help your people see new angles, opportunities, and possibilities. Aim to understand them and elevate them in every conversation. It's important to focus your attention and be perceived as focusing your attention, so don't check your phone, smartwatch, or other notifications while you are in one-on-one conversations and meetings.

Observations

It's impossible for a human to be completely objective. We bring our assumptions, inferences, biases, dreams, fears, fatigue, and imperfections to every situation. That said, you need to develop the skill of observation, which requires the intention to be as objective as possible.

Observations are what you actually see, hear, and notice. For example, you might notice that someone arrived at the meeting ten minutes late and did not apologize when entering the meeting.

In contrast, assumptions are things we accept to be true without proof. For example, you might think that because the person was late and did not apologize, they don't respect their teammates. Importantly, you cannot be sure from your observation that the person does not respect their teammates. This is an assumption.

Using observations and assumptions to reach conclusions leads to inferences. For example, you might infer that the person who was late and did not apologize doesn't respect their teammates and must be thinking about leaving your organization.

It's natural to make assumptions and inferences, but focus instead on observations to increase performance, create the conditions for security, and facilitate growth. For example, when someone is not making progress on their goals, focus on what actually happened or didn't happen. Avoid assumptions or inferences about them, their competency, or their level of effort.

Observation: "You didn't follow our sales process on these three accounts."

Assumption or inference: "You are careless and lazy."

Observation: "The team found two preventable severity-one bugs in your last PR."

Assumption or inference: "You don't care about quality anymore."

Observation: "We agreed that you would document our onboarding process, but you didn't."

Assumption or inference: "I can't trust you with anything important."

Observation: "You and I talked before about how you talk over people, but you've continued to do it."

Assumption or inference: "You don't respect me or your colleagues."

Observation: "We agreed that you would talk directly to him about the issue, but you talked with other colleagues first."

Assumption or inference: "You prefer gossip to results."

As I wrote these, I was reminded of how easily and naturally we create assumptions and inferences! As humans, we seem to prefer explanations and backstories over observations. Sharing observations leads to better conversations and improvements. Assumptions and inferences lead to defensiveness and frustration. Frequently ask yourself whether you are observing, assuming, or inferring.

Listening

Listening requires intentionally focusing your attention on the conversation. Remember the spotlight. It applies to your hearing as well. Sometimes I imagine the spotlight of my attention shining on a person like they are acting on a Broadway stage.

Listening effectively can involve eye contact, emotion, and body language. Of course, if you are uncomfortable with eye contact (as I am sometimes), do the best you can. Emotion and body language involve your facial expression and the position of your arms and hands. Body language should be open to encourage openness—for example, don't cross your arms, and be sure to orient your body toward the person who is talking. Your facial expression is important as well. An ill-timed frown or scowl can reduce the openness of a conversation.

Your tone also matters. Compare a welcoming, authentic "As your manager, I'm here to support you" to an obligatory, eyes-starting-to-roll "As your manager, I'm here to support you."

Three of the most powerful listening techniques I've learned are from a qualitative researcher I used to work with and Chris Voss, a former top FBI negotiator who wrote *Never Split the Difference*.

Silence: When someone else stops talking, don't feel like you need to start. This gives both of you time to think and reflect. Fight the natural urge to start talking right away. Allow seconds of silence to pass. This encourages the other person to continue sharing.

Labeling: Say, "It seems like..." or "It sounds like..." and then repeat an important part of what they said. This shows that you are listening and attempting to understand. If your label is wrong, the other person will clarify, and you can attempt to label again. For example, after hearing the previous three sentences, you might say, "It seems like labeling shows you are attempting to understand."

Mirroring: Repeat one to three important words with a slightly raised inflection in your voice to suggest a question. For example, you might respond, "Suggest a question?" after hearing the previous sentence. Mirroring shows that you are listening and curious.

Silence, labeling, and mirroring will immediately make you a better listener, which will deepen the connection you have with your people and colleagues.

Critically, properly document your conversations. This helps avoid awkward "Tell me the name of the dog that you previously described to me as your soulmate for the fifth time" situations. Show that you care by taking a genuine interest in who they are as people, not just as employees. Everyone forgets names and details from time to time. Apologize, and keep making an obvious effort. Make notes about your people's dreams, fears, strengths, weaknesses, values, favorite drink, dietary needs and preferences, and other important details about them. A tactic I use is adding the names of partners, kids, and pets to people's contact info in my phone.

Questions

Questions are foundational to meaningful conversations and high-quality relationships and can help establish that you care and are here to support your people. Genuinely asking, "How are you today?" can lead to an important conversation about the need for improved work-life integration or support on improving the relationship between two colleagues.

Questions show curiosity. Asking questions helps your people learn to think for themselves and feel a greater sense of ownership and buy-in around agreements and next steps. To facilitate better problem-solving, ask simple, open-ended questions such as "What have you tried so far?" "What do you really want to accomplish?" and "What might be in your way?" to help clarify thinking without giving advice.

A powerful line of questioning is "What do you want?" followed by "What do you really want?" and other clarifying questions. A fantastic executive coach I know once said he could have entire coaching sessions about this line of questions. Understanding what your people want helps you relate to them and understand where they are coming from.

Another important question for managers to reflect on is "What's in it for them?" Often, organizations expect so much, especially from top performers and people who are truly committed to the organization. Your people have their own needs and aspirations. Clarify the connection between their needs and the organization's needs. It's important to recognize people's accomplishments and efforts and remind them about their impact on themselves.

Use questions to celebrate wins and progress using active constructive responding. "Tell me more!" and "How are you going to celebrate?" are powerful ways to expand the positive impact of good news. You can also use questions to better understand what's going well to explore wins and what can be improved to facilitate learning.

EMPATHY

Empathy is foundational not only for managers but for humans in general. It is central to deepening relationships and serving others with your support and guidance.

Empathy is a deep understanding of the other person and their aspirations, problems, capabilities, and limitations, and it requires the ability to see the world from other people's perspectives. In other words, think about them in their world, not you, not your world. This is different from seeing the world from their vantage point but with your own experiences, expertise, and resources to guide you. It's different than thinking about them in your world. Understand how they are seeing the situation: it's them in their world, not you, not your world. I'm repeating this because this lesson took me a while to learn myself. At first, I naturally thought of myself in the world of others, not them in their world.

Many managers are promoted to manager roles because they excel as individual contributors, which can lead to situations where you think you know the right thing to do because you have been in what seems like a similar situation before. Remember that situations are almost always more complicated than they seem from an outsider's perspective. This is why you have regular coaching conversations with your people where you help them think about the priorities and challenges they are facing.

It's hard to avoid giving advice when it seems like you've been there before. Empathy involves thinking about context when communicating with your people. What's going on in their lives at work and beyond? What's happening with your team and your organization? Has anything changed about your market, industry, or economy? Think about your people as whole people within the context of accomplishments, failures, stressors, and everything else going on in their lives.

Empathy requires curiosity. Making assumptions and giving advice is natural for many managers. Sometimes, advice and clear redirection are appropriate. However, the greater opportunity is compassion and curiosity expressed through questions.

There are a few common obstacles to empathy. Many people attempt to solve problems immediately without first feeling with the person.

Often, people accidentally dismiss or minimize emotions by pointing out how things could be worse. People often feel for the person (sympathy) versus feeling with the person (empathy). Compassion involves believing in your people and their ability to accomplish their goals. It's about having a personal growth mindset—a belief that people can learn and grow throughout their lives—about yourself and others. It also requires acknowledging that no one is perfect.

Empathy isn't just for when things are going wrong; it also matters when things are going well and no one notices or seems to care. People need more than a paycheck to live fulfilling lives. Develop a deep understanding of your people, what they want to accomplish, and what's in their way so you can support them on their journey to a meaningful, fulfilling life. Recognize, encourage, and celebrate them along the way.

AGREEMENTS

Agreements are an absolutely critical part of being an effective manager and member of your organization. Agreements are when two or more people decide who will do what by when. You can also have agreements with others that always apply, such as an agreement to communicate with kindness. When you think about agreements this simply, you realize that you may have hundreds of agreements at any given time.

Agreements are an improvement on expectations for a number of reasons. Expectations are often unclear, while agreements provide clarity. Most people do not aspire to meet expectations. There is rarely delight in merely meeting expectations. However, people want to honor their word when they create an agreement. Fulfilling agreements deepens trust and strengthens relationships.

When creating clear agreements, make sure to define who, what, and when. This means a specific person is responsible for a specific outcome or action by a specific deadline or date.

Note that a deadline cannot move because there's a meaningful reason for the deadline, such as an industry event or customer meeting. A date is more flexible. Make sure that everyone involved in an agreement understands whether the when is a deadline or a date. I much prefer aligning agreements against deadlines. For example, when I was part of launching a community, I created a public, cross-functional launch event and publicized it. This launch event and publicity changed a date to a deadline. And we launched on time!

Conscious Leadership Group has a brilliant recommendation: only agree when your head, heart, and gut create a "full-body yes." Many people avoid saying no, so beware of the "fake yes," when you avoid the near-term discomfort of saying no without an intention to fulfill the agreement.

Aim to keep 90 percent or more of your agreements. This is especially important because your agreements make and break trust with your people, and broken trust is hard to repair. If you need to renegotiate an agreement, talk with the other person or people about it right away. Share your 90 percent goal with your people, and ask them to help hold you accountable. If you do break an agreement, intentionally or unintentionally, have a conversation immediately. Apologize if appropriate, and do better next time. Apologies are about the person you harmed, not about you. Say, "I'm sorry for [what I did], and I will [what I will do] in the future." Meaningful apologies take responsibility for the harm caused and create agreements for the future.

You and your people should also know what your most important agreements are. If everything is a high priority, people won't know where to focus.

Here are a few challenges that I've observed related to agreements. I've personally done everything on this list before, so please accept that we are all masterpieces and works in progress:

- Too many agreements: saying yes to too many things

- Unclear agreements: saying, "Yes, let's do this," or "Yes, this sounds great," without defining what "this" is

- The pain-avoidant fake yes: saying yes to avoid saying no to someone you care about or feel like you can't say no to, even though you know you can't or probably won't fulfill the agreement

- Lack of context: A situation changes, but an agreement isn't renegotiated.

- Different understandings of the agreement: saying, "I'll do that," but not fully committing when the other person feels there's an agreement

- An "I can't trust you anymore" reaction to a single broken agreement: It's important to create clear agreements but also realize that we're all imperfect.

- The "don't they understand how busy I am" fake apology: If you break an agreement, apologize and do better next time. People rightfully expect more from you because you are a manager and leader.

It's hard to keep track of your agreements. You have agreements with your organization through your goals. You have agreements with your manager. You have agreements with your peers. You have agreements with your people. You have agreements in other areas of your life. Fulfilling your agreements creates trust. Not fulfilling these agreements breaks trust.

Say no when you need to. Healthy selfishness and boundaries are a must for managers. Make sure you have enough time for ongoing agreements such as one-on-one meetings, sharing feedback, and your own deep work. Renegotiate agreements when you need to. This should happen rarely, but it will happen. Apologize and immediately do better when you break an agreement. Doing better often means saying yes only to the most important things.

A great first step when looking to fulfill agreements is conducting an agreement audit. Create a list of every agreement you're involved in and who will do what by when for each agreement. Include agreements where you are accountable to someone else and where someone else is accountable to you. Once you've created a list of every agreement, take the following steps:

- Prioritize your agreements based on performance, security, and growth needs.

- For any agreement that is past due, apologize and renegotiate.

- For any agreement that doesn't seem important anymore or needs a deadline/date change, renegotiate the agreement.

- For any agreement that you're not a full-body yes to, renegotiate the agreement and consider eliminating it.

The effort and potential short-term pain associated with this agreement audit will help you become more mindful of your agreements. Make sure you are giving a present, full-body yes instead of a fake yes. The trust of your people and your success depend on it.

PART 2

THE FIVE PRACTICES

The five practices are the ways you demonstrate presence and empathy as you fulfill agreements in support of increased performance, safety, and growth. These practices will amplify your positive influence and increase the visibility of your team's accomplishments as well as your own. If you want to be promoted as a people leader, you have to have a high-performing team and multiply your influence through your team, your peers, and others. These practices combine into a simple framework that is critical to your management and leadership approaches.

The five practices are prioritized goals, feedback, one-on-ones, decision-making, and collaboration. You might be thinking, *I am already too busy. How am I going to add new practices when I'm already working some nights and weekends?* These practices will save you time because you will be managing what matters. You will create a rhythm of higher performance, more security, and increased growth for your people because you'll identify problems earlier, make better decisions, and waste less time. You will regularly provide feedback and coaching about what's most important, what's going well, and what can be improved so your people won't interrupt you with avoidable questions every day. Using these five practices, you will ensure that you and your people are working on what's most important, and you'll create momentum for what matters in your organization.

Chapter 4

Prioritized Goals

Prioritized goals help you and your team understand where to focus your energy and efforts. Without prioritized goals, your people may waste time working on the wrong things. If you provide your people with prioritized goals, you will increase performance and save yourself the ongoing headaches of having to help your people make prioritization decisions and people making them on their own.

Many, if not most, organizations have goals. Far fewer organizations have prioritized goals. Without prioritized goals, it's challenging to understand how to prioritize your energy and efforts. For example, is revenue or gross margin more important to your organization? Are you moving fast and breaking things or aiming to discover all your bugs before you ship anything? Should your customer support teams focus on delighting your customers with over-the-top service or responding as quickly as possible to cover more accounts? Is enabling your sales team or building your brand more important? In most organizations, the answer to each of these questions is both. While both things are important, the question is which one is more important. If you don't provide the relative importance to your people, you are stranding them as they make decisions, have meetings, and allocate resources.

A simple definition of a goal is what you want to accomplish. Whichever goals framework you and your organization choose to use, make sure you clearly define your terms and process. For example, are your goals committed, aspirational, or a combination of both? How many goals should someone have?

Whenever possible, your prioritized goals should focus on outcomes and the leading indicators of those outcomes. Too many organizations only use lagging indicators such as quarterly revenue as goals, especially at the executive level. If you only prioritize and review lagging indicators, you are trying to drive your team forward, looking only in the rearview mirror. It's too late to influence a lagging indicator unless you are measuring leading indicators and milestones along the way.

Your process matters as well. For example, how often do you review and update your goals? What happens to your goals if the context around your organization changes? How do your goals relate to your performance review and promotion processes?

As you probably expect, my recommendation is to keep goals simple. You and your team should cocreate and prioritize individual goals to align with organizational goals and values. When your people are involved in your goal-setting process, a higher level of commitment follows. Aim for one to five goals, and make sure to prioritize them and label them as committed or aspirational.

For example, one of an organization's goals may be to increase revenue to $253 million by the end of the year. An individual on a sales team may have a committed quarterly goal of $400,000 in new revenue in support of this organizational goal, with an aspirational quarterly goal of $450,000. Someone in customer success may have a 94 percent committed and 97 percent aspirational customer retention goal in support of this organizational goal. Someone on the legal team might have a committed goal to reduce contract redline turnaround times to one business day and an aspirational goal of less than four business hours for deals over a certain size.

Prioritized goals should not be a set-it-and-forget-it practice. Discuss progress against goals during your one-on-one meetings at least twice per month and during your weekly team meeting. Your people should spend around 90 percent of their time focused on their goals. This helps address the "But what about the time I spend doing ____?" concern from your people. Importantly, your prioritized goals should motivate and inspire your people because they should reflect the meaningful work those people do. It's your responsibility to ensure that people know their work is important.

At a minimum, a person's goals should reflect the quantity, quality, and complexity of their work. Make sure you balance quality, quantity, and complexity for each of your people. Decide the right balance for your team and each of your people, and remember to enable autonomy. People want freedom and flexibility to accomplish what they need to accomplish, so make sure to measure outcomes, not activity or availability. You want your people to think of new ways to do their jobs more effectively with less effort.

Your people need prioritized goals. You need performance from your people. Because you want to manage what matters, you want to give your people autonomy. You can't do this if you have to tell them what matters most over and over again. This wastes your time and their time.

When creating prioritized goals, avoid these mistakes:

- Not prioritizing goals (alarmingly common)

- Trying to document everything as a goal, objective, key result, etc.

- Using goals and key results as a to-do list, not a list of what matters most

- Setting goals and not talking about them again until review time six months or a year later

- Focusing only on lagging indicators of individual, team, and organizational performance

- Not updating goals when significant things change

- Creating unclear organizational goals

- Setting goals that are too easy

- Setting goals that can't be measured

- Setting goals that are ambiguous

- Getting lost in a complicated goal-setting process that takes months instead of managing what matters

To help your people prioritize their goals, you and your organization should provide a vision statement, picture, annual goals, and short-term goals.

The vision statement is a long-term, clear, meaningful description of the change that your organization wants to bring into the world. The vision statement should look at least ten years in the future, with a shared understanding of what it means. Avoid empty corporate-speak, and create something motivating and inspiring. Great examples include Alzheimer's Association's "A world without Alzheimer's disease" and Disney's "To entertain, inform, and inspire people around the globe through the power of unparalleled storytelling, reflecting the iconic brands, creative minds, and innovative technologies that make ours the world's premier entertainment company."

The picture is a medium-term, clear, meaningful description of what your organization will look like. Aim for three years in the future, and make sure you answer the important question of "What's in it for me?" Note this doesn't mean just focusing on your financial goals. It could mean being part of a community, participating in a movement, or feeling connected to something larger than yourself. The picture should be at least five hundred words long to provide sufficient clarity.

Test the power of your vision statement and picture with people to gather feedback and improve them before you share them with your entire team or organization.

Annual goals should reflect your organization's priorities for this year, and short-term goals should reflect your organization's priorities for this quarter.

If your organization doesn't provide a vision statement, picture, annual goals, and short-term goals, you can advocate for these important needs (please create them if you are a CEO or on the senior leadership team), or you can create placeholders that are relevant for your team. For example, if your organization doesn't have a vision statement, you can create a simple one for your team that reflects the power and importance of your team's work. This will help your people feel seen and valued and save them hours of wondering, *Why am I spending my time and talents working for this organization?*

If your organization doesn't have prioritized annual goals, you can create and prioritize goals for your people as they relate to your team's work. For example, I have started a few new teams in my career where my new hire and I were the entire team, tasked with determining whether what we were doing was valuable enough to necessitate additional investments and people. On one of these teams of two, only a handful of companies anywhere in the world were doing what we were doing. We combined our understanding of what our customers needed from us and where our nascent field was headed into a vision statement that guided our strategy and helped us educate our organization about what we were doing and why.

Ensure that you are requiring intentional growth from your people. Don't settle for ambiguous growth goals like "learn about marketing." Agree that your team member will read three classic books on marketing, subscribe and listen to a favorite marketing podcast, earn a certification, or shadow someone for a day and present to your team about what they learned and how it can benefit you and your team. Half-hearted attempts don't lead to growth.

GOALS AND MOTIVATION

As you are creating and prioritizing your goals, it's important to communicate the why behind them. Your people need work that matters—and to believe that their work matters. This means clearly communicating how their work positively impacts your organization's goals, their colleagues, your customers, and the world. Everyone has what I call a motivational signature that is unique and may change over time. Here are some common whole-person needs included in a motivational signature:

- Achievement: accomplishing things that matter

- Autonomy: freedom and flexibility to be themselves

- Belonging/Community: connecting deeply with others

- Benefits: fundamental needs such as health insurance, paid sick leave, and vacation time for renewal

- Impact: positively influencing others and the world

- Learning: developing new skills and abilities

- Meaning/Purpose: being part of something larger than themselves

- Money/Compensation: acquiring the means to fulfill needs and wants

- Self-Actualization: becoming their greatest selves

- Status: increasing one's relative positioning

Understand and honor the motivational signatures of the people on your team. Try to determine someone's motivational signature in your first or second one-on-one meeting with them or, even better, during the interview process. Take notes about what matters to your people, and update your understanding of their motivational signature as it changes.

Don't expect other people to have the same motivational signature that you do. Use the list above to understand and honor different motivational signatures. It's okay for your people to be motivated by money. Not everyone needs to work just for meaning and purpose, even at an organization aiming to change the world. Make it safe for people to express their authentic motivational signatures. A high-performing engineer once told me they just wanted to solve really hard problems. A salesperson shared that they loved the accountability and freedom that came from running their own business within our business.

Knowing your people's motivational signatures allows you to properly motivate them by recognizing meaningful progress and savoring wins. There are a variety of ways to celebrate wins. Understand the celebration that makes sense for your people. For example, someone motivated by self-actualization may appreciate a sponsored session with a strengths coach. Someone motivated by autonomy may appreciate a week to pursue a passion project. Someone motivated by status may appreciate a title change or the opportunity to pursue a certification. A team that has spent sixty hours a week together for the past four months to hit a critical deadline may appreciate some time apart instead of a team party right away. Understand what matters to your people so you can motivate and recognize them.

Get personal with your celebrations. Mix money and extra vacation time with experiences and gifts. Almost everyone receives a digital paycheck, so extra money sometimes goes unnoticed. Enable an experience instead. Buy someone front-row tickets to a concert or sporting event. Buy someone a personalized bottle of their favorite bourbon. One of my favorite celebrations was sending someone on their "dream date night" with their partner (with a $500 limit). The celebration was memorable and led to a great conversation about what they decided to do together, plus we honored the support that their spouse gave them while they were working hard.

HOW TO HELP YOUR PEOPLE ACHIEVE THEIR GOALS

One of your most important responsibilities is helping your people achieve their goals. Clear values help your people understand how they are expected to operate, collaborate, and contribute. Your values are values because they matter to your organization. Focus on how your people achieve their goals from a values perspective. For example, a salesperson who hits their quota by misleading customers about your product's functionality is achieving their goal but failing the organization. Similarly, a software engineer who inflates the estimates of their projects may hit a quantity goal but is playing a deceptive game rather than doing their best for your organization.

Performance should be about what people accomplish and how they accomplish it. Lightweight, effective processes can amplify your people's impact. Entire books have been written about individual, team, and organizational productivity. Some approaches have an almost religious following.

Here are five simple, must-do practices related to productivity:

Daily Prioritization

Daily prioritization is as simple as reviewing your prioritized goals and asking yourself, "What is the most important thing I must do today to make progress?" Complete and repeat. Help your people adopt this simple, powerful practice. Doing something that matters every day is a great way to stay motivated. Encourage your people to break their prioritized goals into chunks so they can make regular progress.

Maker Time

Maker time is about blocking time on your calendar to do deep work without interruptions. This might be challenging because managers are often invited to an overwhelming number of meetings. To create maker time, conduct a regular meeting audit where you improve or eliminate unnecessary meetings, and block time on your calendar where you can only be interrupted for emergencies.

Meaningful Meetings

Meaningful meetings involve meeting for specific reasons, holding everyone accountable for participation in the meeting, and creating agreements based on what happens in the meeting. Help your organization improve the quality and productivity of meetings by asking the goal of each meeting you attend. Regularly audit your calendar and meetings. Cancel meetings that are unnecessary. Shorten meetings that can be shortened. Keep your meetings active, fast, and energetic. Start from a blank calendar, and think about the meetings you actually need to increase performance, security, and growth.

Ongoing Measurement

Ongoing measurement helps your people receive feedback on their progress from the work itself. For example, how many tickets have been resolved, stories completed, opportunities created, or deals won? Create a scoreboard of leading and lagging performance metrics that's easy to see, and reference it regularly. Your people should have an informed perspective on their performance based on the metrics your team tracks. Their work and its output should provide your people with valuable feedback.

Regular Learning

Regular learning should happen during your one-on-one meetings, team meetings, and review processes. Create ceremonies where you talk about what's going well and what can be improved. In addition, your people should always be learning and growing. The challenging, meaningful work you are giving them should result in growth. The competition of their self-development goals should result in growth. Remember that most people crave variety, novelty, and growth in their work.

GETTING STARTED WITH PRIORITIZED GOALS

To get started, determine what your organization's prioritized goals are. If your organization doesn't have prioritized goals, ask your leadership to prioritize your organization's goals, and rank them for your people while you wait for an answer. Your people need to know what's most important for your organization.

Next, determine the most important outcomes you and your team are accountable for. The importance level is the relationship to your organization's prioritized goals.

Share the list of prioritized organizational and team goals with your people, and then cocreate each person's goals with them. I prefer to let people create a draft of their goals on their own before we collaborate so they have as much autonomy as possible while still honoring what our organization needs from us. You want your people to feel bought into their goals. Participation increases buy-in and improves the quality of goals.

Focus goals on the most important outcomes that will occur over the next three, six, or twelve months. Outcomes are what matters, not activities or availability, so don't get obsessed with how an outcome will be achieved. Involve your people in creating the how—the plans for achieving the goals.

Help your people focus by limiting them to one to three goals. Your people should be able to remember their goals without looking them up.

Write each goal so it will be clear when the goal is completed. Quantify the goal if possible, and ensure that there's no ambiguity about what's expected.

Prioritize the goals. Make sure your people clearly understand what's most important so they can maximize their impact. This might be the most important part of leadership.

Create agreements around the prioritized goals. Clearly agree on who will do what by when. You are accountable for holding your people accountable. If you don't hold your people accountable, you are showing them that their work doesn't matter.

Chapter 5

Feedback

You cannot be a successful manager without the ability to give and receive feedback. When many people hear the word "feedback," they think of critique. However, feedback should include recognition, encouragement, observations, advice, and redirection. You have an opportunity to meaningfully impact your people and their work through the feedback you provide.

Also, make sure to receive feedback well, no matter how it's given. While this doesn't mean that you should accept abusive or hostile language, sometimes people will share valuable learnings and insights with you in an imperfect way. It's a mistake to miss an opportunity to learn and grow just because someone is impolite, angry, or frustrated. Often, emotional feedback contains the greatest lessons because many emotional exchanges suggest that something deeper is happening. I've spent years in the field talking to users and customers. Having someone tell you to your face that your product sucks can lead to insight if you are open and curious about why they said it.

RECOGNITION

Recognition involves noticing effort, progress, and accomplishments. Recognizing people as they make meaningful progress on meaningful work nourishes motivation, so ensure that your people know that their effort, progress, and accomplishments matter.

When done poorly, recognition can be demotivating. For example, a casual "good job" at the completion of a two-hundred-hour effort done on an accelerated timeline will likely frustrate the person, not motivate them. Ensure that the recognition and rewards align with the level of effort invested. If someone works nights and weekends for a month to meet a client deadline, thank them personally, give them extra vacation time, and remember this level of commitment during their next review.

It's easy to become immersed in your own prioritized goals and lose appreciation for the efforts of your people. Sometimes, it even feels rational because "we're all in this together, aren't we?" Other times, you might forget that something that would be simple for you is challenging for someone with less experience than you have. No matter the reason, forgetting to appreciate your people can damage your relationship with them.

Don't underestimate the power of saying, "Thank you! What you did matters so much because..."

Here are seven simple techniques to ensure you recognize your people:

- Create and regularly review a dashboard that clearly describes progress and wins. Ensure that you appreciate the progress your people are making on what matters most to your organization. Review leading and lagging indicators.

- Create ceremonies with individuals on your team where you talk about what's going well. By talking about progress and wins during your one-on-ones, you are building the habit of seeing and appreciating the work of people on your team.

- Get your team involved. At least once per month, have team-level retrospectives where you talk about what's going well and what can be improved.

- Strengths spotting involves labeling, describing, and appreciating someone's strengths. Strengths are areas of natural talent that someone has invested in. Even if you don't know someone's strengths from a formal assessment, you can still reflect on what their strengths may be. Give each strength a name, and add detail. For example, you may label someone's strength as strategic thinking, which you describe as the ability to see the right plan even when things are complex. To show them you appreciate that strength, you might thank them and describe the impact. For example, "I appreciate your contributions as a strategic thinker because you know the right next step even when things change and we aren't sure what to do. This gives the team confidence and direction."

- Active constructive responding is a simple yet magical way to deepen connections by celebrating wins and good news. You should be emotionally engaged through your words, tone, and body language and have a meaningful conversation instead of a simple "nice work!" This helps build the other person up. An example of active constructive responding might be: "Congratulations! I know you've worked so hard on that project. Tell me more about how you're going to celebrate!" Don't passively say, "That's great." and move to the next topic. Don't be destructive by saying, "Congratulations! You'll never get to take a real vacation again." Smile. Ask questions. Take a few moments to celebrate them.

- Reminders, cues, and ceremonies are important for managers and leaders. It's easy to get deeply involved in a project or unexpected emergency and realize you haven't appreciated your people in a few weeks. Technology can remind people to appreciate each other. In addition, you can add recurring meetings to your calendar called "Recognize and Savor" to remind you to appreciate your people and yourself. Include recognition in your one-on-one and retrospective checklists.

- In addition to ongoing and impromptu feedback, performance reviews should recognize wins, growth, and effort. It's natural to focus on where people came up short, but ensure that you are also celebrating wins and identifying opportunities for improved performance.

ENCOURAGEMENT

Encouragement allows managers to be a positive influence on others, especially when things are in progress, uncertain, or not going well. Encouragement reminds people that they are masterpieces and works in progress with tremendous possibility. Nourish your people with encouragement to increase performance, create safety, and facilitate growth.

Here are ten ways you can increase the power of your encouragement:

- Honor the person's feelings and emotions. The person you are attempting to encourage may be frustrated or angry. Listen to them. Feel with them. Don't trivialize how they are feeling with a well-intended "It's not a big deal" or "It will be okay."

- Empathize by thinking deeply about them in their world. Remember: them in their world, not you, not your world. You are encouraging a person with hopes, dreams, fears, and stressors. It's important to consider the whole person, including their context.

- Be specific when you give encouragement. Don't rely only on generic statements like "You can do it!" Give specific reasons and examples of their capabilities.

- Be honest and credible. Be optimistic about what's possible. Tell the truth courageously and compassionately when things are going poorly.

- Remind them that they matter to you and are valued. Remind them that you care about them as a person. Consistently demonstrate that your people matter to you through your words and actions.

- Attempt to create psychological safety. Remind them that mistakes are an opportunity to learn. Regularly talk about what's going well for you and what can be improved about you to normalize imperfection.

- Have a personal growth mindset, and encourage them to have one as well. Remind them that they can grow, learn, and evolve throughout their entire life. Believe in your people. If you don't, reflect on why, and create a plan for restoring that belief immediately.

- Remind them of their progress and learning. You can build resilience by seeing and appreciating progress.

- Remind them about their strengths and the tremendous impact they can have. Know your people's strengths and weaknesses, as well as your own.

- Remind them that they matter, and so does their work. Reconnect them to the importance of what they do. It's your responsibility to remind your people regularly that their work is important.

OBSERVATIONS

Observations involve bringing attention to something you have seen, heard, or noticed. Become an expert at observing what actually happened, while minimizing your own assumptions, inferences, judgments, and biases. Regularly sharing observations creates a mutual understanding of performance, security, and growth. You can help others by sharing your observations as part of an intentional, safe conversation. Here's a step-by-step guide to effectively and safely sharing your observations:

Before the Conversation

- Create a clear intention for the conversation.

- Focus on observations, data, and examples. Specifically, what do you want to share?

- Think about what you want to accomplish. What are you hoping starts, stops, or continues?

- Focus on how this conversation will build on what makes this person great. How will this conversation make the other person stronger, happier, or more aware?

- Decide how you will help them prepare for this conversation. How will you avoid surprising them, especially when sharing redirection?

- Determine the right place for this conversation. Should the conversation be private?

- Make sure there's enough time and mental space for this conversation. Conversations take time.

During the Conversation

- Remember to keep your body language open and be fully present.

- Determine the right tone for this feedback. Even redirection can be delivered with kindness and empathy.

- Invite them to share their thoughts and feelings.

- Focus on what really happened, not assumptions or inferences about the person. What are specific things you have seen, heard, or noticed?

- Be specific and say what you really need to say.

- Think about them in their situation, not you in their situation.

- Ask questions to understand their perspective and the context around the situation. Remember that no one can be fully objective.

After the Conversation

- Remind the other person that people can grow, change, and learn.

- Invite them into the conversation about next steps, and cocreate a plan.

- Remind them of agreements—who is responsible for what and by when. Determine how you will measure change.

ADVICE

Advice is a recommendation for a future action. It can be a useful tool for managers but should be used infrequently. Unfortunately, many managers and leaders naturally lean into advice rather than observations and questions. Michael Bungay Stanier's book *The Advice Trap: Be Humble, Stay Curious, & Change the Way You Lead Forever* calls this "the advice monster," or that natural human tendency to believe that you are sharing the best answer. In most circumstances, managers should ask questions and share observations to support and challenge their people, build connections, create better solutions, and increase buy-in.

That said, sometimes your people may need your advice. You may have tried sharing observations and asking questions without the needed change in performance or behavior. You may have a potentially great idea to share. One of your team members may insist on hearing what you would do in a particular situation.

Here are eight keys to giving useful advice:

- Seek to understand the situation. Ask questions about what the person wants to accomplish and what's in their way. Understand the problem thoroughly before you offer a potential solution.

- Help the person see the situation from a different perspective and within a larger context. As a manager and leader, you have a different vantage point than your people.

- Consider sharing advice about things to think about versus things to do. This helps people learn to think more independently.

- Have a conversation about possible approaches rather than just sharing an idea. Hearing their thoughts on your advice may help you better understand the situation and improve your guidance.

- Keep it short and simple. Many managers and leaders seem to lose the ability to be succinct.

- Tell a relevant story if possible. People learn from and remember stories.

- Make it clear you are giving advice versus redirection. Advice is a suggestion. Redirection describes a necessary change in performance or behavior. It's your responsibility to communicate the difference and create the right agreements.

- Be respectful. Remember there's a capable person on the receiving end of your advice. Avoid the word "easy." If the problem were easy to solve, the person most likely would have solved it.

As someone whose natural inclination is sharing ideas, I need to watch out for the advice monster and remind myself that I am often coaching (guiding others), not consulting (finding and sharing the answer). To balance sharing ideas and enabling autonomy, a phrase I use frequently is "I would consider..." which focuses my comments on things to think about and possible approaches to take. For example, I might say, "I would consider looking at our organizational chart to think through who all of your stakeholders are." This can lead to a conversation and have a different effect than saying, "Make sure you talk to our implementation and support teams." There's buy-in when people are involved in creating their plans. There's a clear distinction between "I would consider" conversations and "You must" conversations. "I would consider" conversations are suggestions, while "You must" conversations create new agreements that must be upheld.

REDIRECTION

Redirection is a required change in output or behavior. It should be reserved for serious situations involving concerns over performance, ethics, policies, or values.

Redirecting your people too often removes their sense of ownership, autonomy, and accountability. Feeling like your manager makes all your decisions for you makes it easy to blame your manager when you don't achieve your prioritized goals.

Many managers struggle with clear redirection. Some managers avoid conflict. Some sugarcoat redirection with praise, making it less serious. Some make it seem like advice or a suggestion to avoid conflict or hurt feelings. Some feel that compassion and candor are mutually exclusive. If you don't provide clear redirection when it's needed, people will be confused about what's expected.

To avoid the most common pitfalls associated with redirection, remember these seven things:

- Frequent feedback: Unless the situation is sudden and unexpected, this should not be the first time you are discussing the need for change. Previous conversations should have included observations and advice.

- Preparation: If you are involved in a situation requiring redirection, follow relevant workplace laws and your company policies. Involve your people/HR and legal teams appropriately and early.

- Conversation: Have an authentic conversation about what happened, the necessary change, and why it's required. People should have the opportunity to share their perspective and ask questions if appropriate. If you don't have all the answers immediately, you can follow up quickly.

- Agreements: Everyone needs to understand who will do what by when. You may need to manage the agreements and provide additional support.

- Accountability: Everyone needs to understand what will happen if the agreements are fulfilled and if they are not.

- Follow-up: Written documentation helps with clarity, accountability, and risk mitigation. Redirection conversations are often emotional on both sides. Written documentation helps everyone remember what was actually said and agreed to.

- Learning: Attempt to learn what, if anything, you could have done differently. For example, did you make the need for change clear? Were the agreements clear from the beginning? Did you provide ongoing feedback? Should you have said something sooner?

If you manage and lead people for any significant amount of time, you will find yourself in situations requiring redirection. This happens even at organizations that win culture awards and have books written about their culture. It's your responsibility to identify when other types of feedback aren't appropriate anymore and provide clear redirection when it's necessary.

REQUESTING AND RECEIVING FEEDBACK

Feedback helps us grow and should be welcomed and invited. It's an opportunity to deepen your connection with another person, identify critical blind spots, and change the trajectory of your career. Feedback impacts my own growth more than anything else. Instead of guessing how I am perceived or how impactful I am as a manager and leader, I proactively and frequently ask, "What's going well?" and "What can be improved?"

Your behavior influences the behavior of your team and all of your stakeholders. By proactively requesting feedback and acting on it when appropriate, you show others that you are striving to improve and that you value their input. Encourage your people to request feedback as well. One simple way to do this is sharing something that you are working to improve and asking for advice.

Many people are afraid of receiving feedback and may act defensively when it is given. I believe almost everyone experiences frustration or defensiveness when receiving feedback, at least from time to time. I know I do, and I have trained thousands of people on feedback. It's natural to think of excuses and explanations for our perceived shortcomings. Don't they know how busy you are? But what about all the other amazing wins you've had? Do they expect you to do everything for them? These are natural responses that we all feel.

I've received some useful but hard-to-take feedback in my career. Someone once told me that one of my products ruined shopping for them and made them start shopping at a competitor's store. Once, I thought I was being exceptionally supportive to a peer leader and was told they thought I was undermining them instead. Someone once told me they believed I thought I already knew all the answers and was only asking for their input because I had to. Receiving this feedback helped me see situations differently and increase my positive impact.

Here are eleven ways to gather valuable feedback:

Your Performance

Look for learning in your own successes and failures. The impact you are having or not having on your organization can provide valuable learnings. For example, you may realize that you are successful when you are responsible for an outcome on your own but unsuccessful when you have to collaborate with others who don't report to you.

Your People's Performance

You can and should have a substantial influence on the success of your people. When your people aren't successful, examine whether you could have supported them more effectively. For example, could you have made their priorities clearer, shared observations earlier, or helped them foresee obstacles? Could you have instilled a greater sense of urgency? Could you have emphasized why they matter and their work matters? When your people are successful, celebrate their success, and look to learn what worked and what didn't. When your people don't achieve their goals, accept that it's a learning opportunity for everyone, including you.

One-on-Ones

When you are fully attentive during your one-on-ones, you'll notice feedback and opportunities for improvement throughout the conversation. Regularly ask questions like "Is there anything I can do to better support you?" and listen for those opportunities. For example, are you giving your people the right amount of freedom and flexibility? Are they stuck and unwilling to admit it? Are they losing their motivation? Are they feeling too busy or guilty to take time off to rest and recover? If you understand whole-person needs and listen actively during one-on-ones, you'll find that people provide feedback about themselves, you, your organization, and the ways you can better support them in every conversation.

Team-Level Retrospectives and Debriefs

Similar to one-on-ones, team-level conversations are full of opportunities for learning and improvement. Questions about what went well, what can be improved, and what should be done differently are gold mines for managers. Don't expect your people to always say, "This is the perfect way for you to support us." Simple questions such as "What went well?" "What can be improved?" and "What should we do differently next time?" can provide even more valuable learnings if you ask about and reflect upon why things were shared.

Clarifying Questions

Ask clarifying questions such as "Why do you think that happened?" and "Could you say a bit more so I can understand?" For example, if someone says a project took a while to get started, asking clarifying questions lets you know why. Was there a perceived lack of goal clarity, role clarity, meaning, focus, leadership, decision-making authority, or something else? You will create a lot of value by hearing what your people actually need and giving it to them, and your people will appreciate you for this. Many impactful people-management behaviors are essentially free. For example, clear prioritization, meaningful work that challenges them and helps them grow, freedom to do their work, recognition when they win and make progress, and support when they run into challenges all just take a small amount of time supported by inexpensive tech and simple processes.

Reviews

When done properly, reviews provide valuable feedback. Feedback should be given continuously and not reserved for reviews. That said, reviews allow you to give and receive summative feedback from a wide, zoomed-out viewpoint. Ongoing feedback is often tactical, but reviews should include both strategic and tactical feedback. Ideally, reviews involve feedback from other team members and peers as well. If you work for a manager who doesn't provide sufficient feedback during reviews, ask for what you need to do well to succeed and grow. If you aren't giving people comprehensive feedback during reviews, start doing so even if it's not required by your organization.

Before or After a Specific Action

Specific actions such as announcing a new strategy provide opportunities to gather input about the proposed change and about the announcement to improve the next one. Simple prompts such as "What's one thing you might change about this?" or "What's one thing I could have done better?" can help your team provide the right amount of feedback. Receive feedback with curiosity and without defensiveness, no matter how it's delivered.

Impromptu Requests

Frequently asking questions like "How could I better support you?" and "Is there anything else you need to be successful?" reminds your people that you care about them. A CEO at a company I used to work for would ask me if there was anything he could do for me at the end of every conversation, even though I didn't report to him. I only asked for a couple of things over a few years, but he followed through when I did. What a way to show support as an executive! If you ask your people what they need and honor agreements you make about providing it, you will build trust with your team.

360s

A 360 review involves feedback from the people on your team, your peers, your management, and other stakeholders. Gathering feedback from all of your stakeholders is important because you may unconsciously show up differently with people at different levels. For example, you may coach your own people well but be perceived as condescending by your peers.

Ask for 360 feedback from up to ten people at a time, and set clear guidelines for the feedback you want to receive. This will allow you to understand themes without being overwhelmed by the feedback. As a coach, I've seen executives I hardly know cry during 360 debriefs as they wonder why their colleagues never shared certain criticisms with them before. Critical feedback can be unexpected and shared with intense emotional language. Help people share useful feedback by reminding them of the intention of the 360 review: to help you learn and grow.

Engagement Surveys

Your organization should regularly ask its people for feedback using engagement surveys and other tools, and it should confidentially share the responses from your team. If your organization doesn't use engagement surveys, they are inexpensive enough that you can invest in them yourself for your team or department. Make sure you ask questions about whole-person needs—performance, security, and growth—and take action on the feedback. Especially the first time you attempt to interpret and act upon engagement survey results, it's extremely helpful to have someone familiar with the questions you asked coach you through the process.

Confidential and Anonymous Means

Even if you are a great manager at a great organization, there may be times people don't feel safe enough to share their honest feedback. Because feedback is data and a gift that helps us learn and grow, we need to provide opportunities for them to share their honest opinions. Having the courage to welcome direct and anonymous feedback is a strong signal sign that a leader is here to help their team and organization succeed and grow.

WHAT TO DO AFTER RECEIVING FEEDBACK

Don't feel like you have to solve the issue or address anything immediately. Acknowledge and honor how the other person is feeling. Thank them for the feedback, and remind them that their input is important. Don't agree to anything too soon. Only say you will follow up if you will.

After the conversation, prioritize the feedback based on importance and urgency. Think about how it relates to performance, security, and growth. Remember that no one is perfect and attempting to change too much at once is most often counterproductive. It's better to make a series of small agreements to show your people growth and progress.

Listening, prioritizing, and agreeing are critical, but they are meaningless without action. Do what you agreed to do by the agreed-upon date. When you take action, thank the person for the feedback again.

When you consider feedback as data rather than directives, focus on learning, and limit the number of agreements you make, you can continuously increase your impact and influence while strengthening your relationships. Too many managers fall into the trap of trying to implement too many ideas and practices from feedback, books, gurus, and podcasts all at once, which can be confusing. Introduce practices to your team intentionally, explaining the reason for the new practice. For example, a simple routine of prioritized goals every quarter, meaningful one-on-ones every two weeks, and a team-level retrospective every month will create an excellent foundation.

Experiment intentionally. You don't have to adopt every practice from every book, podcast, or social post. If you try something but it doesn't work, don't be afraid to eliminate it. I worked with a client once who realized their monthly department meeting duplicated what everyone already knew from team meetings. They made it a monthly "wins and learnings" email with a quarterly department meeting instead. Everyone was happy to have a meeting removed from their calendar. Eliminating things makes room for improvement. Many of us, including me, naturally think create, not curate. Schedule time and ceremonies for curation, and remove what's not working.

As you are attempting to change habits and introduce new behaviors based on feedback, aim to use tools, technology, and ceremonies in combination. Tools are decision-making frameworks, canvases, and meeting templates. Tools help you capitalize on other people's learnings to save time. Technology includes software for aligning around company goals, providing ongoing feedback, and recognizing colleagues. Technology can scale your impact as a meaningful manager. Ceremonies include retrospectives, one-on-ones, and reviews. Ceremonies help you and your team make progress toward your goals and cultivate high-quality connections. Ideally, managers should partner with their HR/people partners as well. Cocreate the right combination of tools, technologies, and ceremonies to increase performance, security, and growth.

Chapter 6

One-on-Ones

One-on-ones are a powerful practice that fosters performance, security, and growth and deepens high-quality connections with your people. One-on-ones are a meeting between two people. Effective one-on-ones should be meaningful, invigorating, restorative conversations where you strengthen and motivate your people by recognizing their progress and effort, coaching them through tough situations, and understanding their needs.

When done properly, one-on-ones can be the most impactful meetings that managers have. One-on-ones empower employees to act autonomously and positively impact your organization. One-on-ones help your people focus on the right prioritized goals. One-on-ones give your people space to talk about issues before they become bigger problems. One-on-ones allow you to guide and coach your people, and they give you the opportunity to recognize, encourage, coach, and advise your people in an ongoing way. One-on-ones help your people feel seen, supported, and valued.

One-on-ones are so important that I have a one-hour one-on-one with each of my people each week. When I managed eight people, I had one day per week dedicated to one-on-ones. We didn't use the entire hour each week, but we never rescheduled unless it was an emergency. My people understood that they mattered to me as people and that their work mattered. A former colleague of mine with twenty direct reports had one-on-ones twice per month with each of their people. This allowed him to guide people in the right direction before smaller issues became larger problems. His team overachieved on their goals, and many of his team members earned promotions ahead of schedule. He also won a top award in our organization of seven hundred people.

Regular, meaningful one-on-ones have a high ROI, save you time, and help you avoid future pain. There are five types of one-on-one meetings to have with your people:

KICKOFF

Your kickoff one-on-one is a sixty-to-ninety-minute conversation where you and your team member share important details about yourselves, your motivations, your preferences, and your nonnegotiables. It's a meeting about both of you, not just them. Both people share and ask questions. You can have a kickoff conversation even if you have been managing someone for a while. If you need a reason to justify having this conversation, you can blame me and this book. You can express your desire to be a manager and leader who focuses on performance, security, and growth. You can apologize for not knowing your people very well and agree to doing better starting with these kickoff meetings. Just have the conversation as soon as possible.

Here are the questions I recommend asking during your kickoff. They should be shared in advance to give both people an opportunity to create authentic, thoughtful responses.

- If you could have anyone as your dinner guest, who would it be and why?

- What are some important things you've learned about yourself in your career?

- What does your ideal work environment look and feel like?

- What are the most important, nonnegotiable things about that environment?

- What's important to you right now personally and professionally?

- What do you want most right now?

- What's your motivational signature? What are a few things that motivate you right now?

- Are your goals clear and prioritized? If not, what's unclear?

- Is your role clear? If not, what's unclear?

- How can I best support you right now?

- What did we agree to today? Who will do what by when?

These questions can be answered in a few sentences each, after some reflection. However, each of these questions can lead to a long, meaningful conversation. For example, the question about the dinner guest might reveal that you have a shared love of the performing arts. Discussing prioritized goals ensures a shared understanding of what's most important and increases the likelihood of success and a fast start. Understanding how you can best support someone lets you know exactly what someone needs from you and creates the foundation for your relationship. Knowing someone's nonnegotiables helps you understand what they value most.

I've been fortunate to have great managers in my career. However, some of them might not have been able to answer these questions about me even after a few years of managing me. Why leave this level of connection to chance? Asking these questions will help you increase performance, security, and growth for your people in a personalized way. Even if you have been managing someone for a year or more, it's worthwhile to have a formal conversation like this. You may not know the answers even after a year. Most managers don't because most managers aren't trained in how to create connections with their people. Also, people evolve and change. Priorities change, motivational signatures change, and so on. This conversation allows you to build and reinforce trust and support your people.

RECURRING

Recurring one-on-ones should occur at least twice per month. Recurring one-on-ones should focus on personal connection, prioritized goals, progress, coaching, feedback, growth, and agreements. Remind your people why they matter to your organization, to you, and to your team. Only cancel one-on-ones in emergency situations.

Be present for your one-on-ones. Because it's finite, attention is one of the most important gifts we can give someone else.

Both people should prepare for recurring one-on-ones. Your team member should prepare updates, questions, and topics to discuss. Review your notes from previous one-on-ones and kickoffs, goals, progress against goals, and any feedback you've received about this team member.

Personal connection can be as simple as a genuine "How are you today?" Someone on a team of mine reminded me of this powerful question that, unfortunately, has become a throw-away. You and your team member are important! Connecting is important! When you ask, "How are you?" ask follow-up questions and refer to previous conversations when appropriate. Feel with them. Share how you are, including when you are struggling or frustrated. Make sure they understand that they are valued as a human and for their contributions to your organization by giving their response your full presence and attention.

Some managers are afraid to coach their people during one-on-ones or have deeper relationships because people can be complicated, and tough situations can arise. If you are in a situation where you aren't sure how to respond, consider saying, "Thank you for sharing that with me. I am here for you. How can I best support you right now?" You might also have to say that you don't know the right answer or what to do but that you will look into it as soon as you can. Ensure that you honor privacy as much as possible while appropriately and discreetly consulting others such as HR and Legal when required.

Prioritized goals ensure you and your people understand what's most important so you know how they should prioritize their energy and time. Discuss prioritized goals and progress toward those goals regularly during one-on-ones. In most organizations, it's easy to get caught up in what's urgent rather than what's important. Notifications and interruptions bombard most people. Colleagues ask for help. Many people have too many goals to keep track of. People spend hours in meetings every week. People get added to projects all the time. One-on-ones are an opportunity to remind both of you what's most important and make adjustments as necessary.

Progress motivates people. People want to make meaningful progress on meaningful work and be seen and recognized for that work. As you discuss prioritized goals, discuss the progress that's being made toward those goals. Make sure you recognize your team member and remind them why their work is important to you and your organization. This can be as simple as saying, "Thanks for closing those three deals! They will really help us hit our revenue target, and it looks like you're on track to achieve your quota. Also, it's inspiring to our organization when we add new customers. I know you worked hard on those!"

Coach your people by asking questions, helping people see situations from different perspectives, and allowing them to create solutions and make decisions with your support. Coaching requires backbone and heart; in fact, there's a great book called *Coaching with Backbone and Heart* by Mary Beth O'Neill that discusses caring deeply about your people as people, not just as team members, and having the courage to give them direct and honest feedback when needed.

Questions are the foundation of excellent coaching. Use these powerful coaching questions regularly:

- What do you want to accomplish? This focuses the conversation on the prioritized goal.

- What's in your way? This helps them talk about problems and allows for follow-up questions.

- Why? This all-purpose question helps uncover causes, not symptoms. Asking why should become a regular habit.

- What have you tried so far? This helps them review their own efforts and see opportunities for improvement and new approaches.

- How might we approach this differently? This ensures they are accountable while allowing you to partner as needed.

- What have you learned during this situation? This facilitates reflection and reminds your team member to keep learning and growing.

- What do you really want? You can have entire coaching sessions just exploring this question.

- Is there anything else you want to discuss? This keeps the conversation open and helps ensure your people feel heard and supported.

- How can I best support you right now? This allows you to partner with your people and cocreate ways to support them while maintaining their accountability. "What can I do for you?" shifts the accountability to you.

- What are we agreeing to? This makes it clear who will do what by when.

A phrase I often use while coaching is "I would consider." This allows me to point out facets of a problem or situation without reducing autonomy. Importantly, the phrase "I would consider" keeps accountability for the decision and the result on them. If you tell your people what they need to accomplish and specifically how to do it, it's easy for them to say, "I was just doing what you told me to do." I also like saying, "This is how I might think through the problem" to give insight into how they can make a better decision in this situation and hopefully future decisions.

"How can I best support you right now?" might be the most important single question you can ask your people regularly. Note the use of the word "support," not "help." Asking for or accepting help can make people feel weak, so they avoid it. By proactively asking how you can support them, you remind them that you are there for them without saying they need help. They are the hero; you are the guide. Ask them to support you as well. Talk about how others support you. This normalizes needing support. Make asking "How can I best support you right now?" a reflex.

Feedback includes recognition, encouragement, observations, advice, and redirection. Recognition involves celebrating wins, progress, effort, and learning. Encouragement reminds people of their power and possibility. Observations are sharing things that you saw, heard, and noticed to start meaningful conversations that strengthen your people. Advice is a recommendation for considering a different approach. Redirection is a required change in behavior. Depending on what you and your team member discuss in your one-on-one, you may need to give more than one type of feedback during the meeting.

If you want to be an effective manager and leader, you have to be able to tell someone when they are not achieving what is necessary or when they are acting in ways that aren't appropriate. Said simply, you cannot hide from challenges and problems. Even if your intentions are to stay positive or care about your people and their feelings, you cannot avoid bringing up issues. Bringing up smaller issues in one-on-ones increases the likelihood that they will stay small.

Your people won't always surface issues, so you may have to. Sharing observations, advice, and redirection when things aren't going well shows care. If someone isn't achieving their goals and you don't say anything, you are saying their work doesn't matter. If someone is acting in a way that doesn't honor your organization's values and you don't say anything, you are endorsing their behavior. If underperformance or the values gap continues, you may have to discipline or fire the person. Isn't the more caring approach telling them what's wrong before reaching that point?

Remember that if you and your people aren't regularly growing, you are falling behind others who are. Your people want to grow by taking on larger challenges, learning new skills, completing courses and certifications, and getting promoted. If your people don't see opportunities for growth, they will likely leave your team or organization. Hold your people accountable for their own growth while also finding opportunities for them to grow. Your people should have prioritized goals for their growth the same way they have prioritized goals for performance. Too many managers allow their people to settle for goals like "learn about marketing." Instead, the goal should be "Reach out to ten possible director or VP of marketing mentors. Meet with a mentor monthly. Read this specific marketing book, and complete this specific online certification." If this seems too specific or challenging, then perhaps your person isn't as interested in their growth or marketing as they claim. Challenge your people in ways that are at the edge of reasonable.

Agreements are commitments about who will do what by when. Many managers do not create clear agreements with their people, leaving ambiguity about what's expected. At the end of each one-on-one, quickly review who will do what by when and any changes to prioritized goals. You need a system for recording agreements you make with others. As you go from meeting to meeting, it's easy to lose track of what you have agreed to. Breaking agreements breaks trust. Fulfilling agreements makes trust. You can't be a meaningful, positive influence on your people without trust.

REVIEWS

Reviews are an opportunity to recognize wins, learn from losses, and help your people grow. If you are conducting recurring one-on-ones regularly, your review process should be a straightforward, no-surprises summary of wins, losses, and feedback you've shared over the last quarter, six months, or year with additional reflection on themes and opportunities for growth. Reviews provide an opportunity to zoom out and reflect on a larger period of time. These reflections can yield insights that you don't see when you are focused on week-to-week progress.

Fairness and perceived fairness are fundamental human needs. Incorporate objective measurement and other sources of data into your reviews to ensure that your expectations are as fair and unbiased as possible. Don't rely solely on your own opinion.

Fully understand the review process, including what you are reviewing, the review process itself, and any decisions based on the reviews. For example, your review process may be input into promotion and compensation decisions, or it may just be about the growth and development of your people. The purpose of your review process should be clear to you and your people. If you don't understand the review process, reach out to your manager and people/HR team and ask questions until you understand.

Before the review process starts, set clear agreements with each of your people. At some organizations, reviews are a frightening, forced-ranking, who-should-we-fire process. I remember a frustrated colleague whose year was summarized as "competent" because that was the word the organization had chosen for the "middle 90 percent" of performers. He was on the edge of top performance and despised being described as merely competent. I hope you don't work at one of those organizations. Eventually, I hope that no one does.

During reviews, make sure to properly recognize wins, growth, and learning. Call attention to the effort required and why the work matters to help your people feel seen and valued. Objective measurements of performance should be reviewed. People can make substantial contributions to an organization's performance, engagement, and culture in areas outside of their defined roles, so also review contributions beyond your people's prioritized goals. If possible, find ways to share verbatim feedback from customers and other stakeholders such as their peers. It's natural for your people to focus on the negative parts of the review. To help nourish motivation and positive energy, honor wins, growth, and learning along the way as well. Losses and learnings from losses should also be reviewed. Talk openly and honestly about where prioritized goals and other agreements weren't met. If you don't, you are saying that those goals and agreements didn't matter. If they didn't matter, why did you prioritize them and agree to them in the first place?

Many managers are afraid to talk about what went wrong, but you are short-changing your growth and the growth of your people if you only talk about wins and what's working. Talking about losses gives you opportunities to learn and improve and shows a high level of care. If your people never lose or fail, it probably means you are risk-averse and not ambitious enough.

Growth can be accelerated during a review. Synthesize feedback, wins, losses, strengths, personal goals, and other data to cocreate a growth plan for each team member. Cocreation is important because you want your team members to feel a sense of ownership and accountability for their own growth. Many team members expect an organization to lay out a menu of options for their advancement, promotion, and career, but this rarely happens. Whether your organization does that or not, you can help your people grow by cocreating a personalized plan with them.

Remember that everyone has likely experienced reviews that seemed unfair and subjective, so reviews are often scary and intimidating. Prepare your people for reviews by sharing everything you can about the process and allowing them to ask questions beforehand. Reviews should be a conversation. Let your people know you want to hear their thoughts. Your reviews should focus on what they accomplished, how they accomplished it, and themes for improvement and growth. Celebrate wins. Learn from wins and losses. After the review, share the results and any agreements made during the review with your team member.

Proactively look for opportunities to improve. Ask your people for feedback about what went well and what can be improved after your review process. Maybe you can update goals more frequently as priorities change or ask questions and provide earlier feedback when things seem off course. Asking your people how you can best support them and then following up with action on any agreements builds trust and rapport.

REAGREEMENT

Reagreements are necessary when priorities change or when someone isn't upholding the agreement. Even with a great team in a great organization, you will likely need to have reagreement conversations with your people sometimes. For example, maybe one of your team members forgot to honor your values when talking to their peers. Maybe you just forgot to create new agreements when someone's prioritized goals changed, or you were assigned a special project and need to adjust agreements you made with some of your people.

Reagreement involves sharing your observations, having a compassionate and candid conversation, and creating new agreements. As you are preparing for a reagreement conversation, ask yourself the following questions:

- Was there an agreement? Often, one person thinks an agreement exists, and the other person does not.

- What was the agreement?

- Why is the agreement important? What does it accomplish for your organization?

- What did you observe? Specifically, what did you see, hear, and notice? Avoid assumptions and inferences.

- Is a new agreement needed, or do you need to uphold the previous agreement? Sometimes you may need someone to uphold the previous agreement with a new deadline or a greater sense of accountability and priority.

- How might the other person see this situation? Think about them in their world, not you or your world.

- What's the context around the situation? For example, have priorities changed? Have goals and roles changed?

Reagreement conversations may be challenging. People will often share explanations and excuses for why agreements were not upheld. Start with observations rather than accusations to facilitate a conversation, and make it clear that you have the shared purpose of helping your organization and its people be successful. Also, make it clear you want to have a conversation, not a monologue.

You may occasionally contribute to an unfulfilled agreement, either intentionally or unintentionally. You may have committed to too many things yourself, or you may have made something sound like a suggestion rather than an agreement. Apologize if necessary, and make sure the agreement is clear this time. Depending on the situation, you may want to use the reagreement conversation to review all your agreements with this specific person to ensure you are both clear.

As soon as you notice a concern about your agreements with someone, schedule a conversation with them. The more you refer to agreements and hold yourself accountable, the more they will. One of your most important responsibilities is making sure your people are working on the right things, and reagreement conversations allow you to double-check on prioritized goals, role clarity, and values.

The simplest way to avoid reagreement conversations is to have clear, prioritized goals and only say yes when you mean it. You have thousands of different ways you can support your team and your organization. Be selective and intentional about the agreements you create. This will help you make the greatest impact and avoid unfulfilled agreements that break trust.

REDIRECTION

Redirection is an urgently or immediately required change in output or behavior. Redirection is required when observations, advice, and reagreements have not led to the necessary changes. You may also need to have a redirection conversation when an unexpected or emergency situation arises—for example, an ethical breach or policy violation. Redirection conversations may involve consulting or involving your people/HR team and legal team. Have these tough conversations when changes in behavior are required, even with people you consider your friends.

Unless there's an unexpected or emergency situation, redirection conversations should not be a surprise to your people. Sometimes, people may claim to be surprised by redirection.

Make sure you have documented attempts to provide feedback and reagree. For example, send an email about what can be improved or new agreements. If you are reaching the point of redirection, other attempts to change behavior should be obvious to you and the other person. Involve your people/HR team as your partner in situations requiring redirection. Your organization likely has policies related to performance and workplace laws that should be consulted as you prepare for a redirection conversation.

Redirection involves conversations about the new agreements that must be completed. After the conversation, provide written documentation about who will do what by when and how you will follow up. There should be no ambiguity about what changes the person needs to make and by when. Ensure that everyone also understands what is at stake. Make sure you give people enough time to change their behavior but require an immediate directional change to reinforce the importance of the necessary changes. You may discover new information during a redirection conversation that requires additional consideration. If this happens, make it clear when you will follow up on the changes that are needed. This should happen as soon as possible and ideally the same day.

CHAPTER 7

DECISION-MAKING

Decisions are important to an organization's success or failure because they determine an organization's vision, mission, values, strategy, planning, execution, and more. Poor decisions cost organizations thousands, millions, or even billions of dollars in wasted time and energy, as well as opportunity costs.

Decision-making is one of the most important skills for managers and leaders. You are accountable for making the best decisions you can with the resources and time you have, but you most often will not have the ideal amount of data and time.

Humility is essential for excellent decision-making. Often, managers and leaders think they have to have all the answers. Many situations feel familiar, and it can be easy to miss nuanced and even material differences, especially as we become more experienced. Managers and leaders need to be comfortable saying, "I don't know," and "We need to look into this more," when appropriate. This helps you make better decisions and models the vulnerability and humility that you want from your people.

Humility reflects the reality of today's complex, ambiguous, and volatile environment. Even specialists cannot know the right answer to every question in their field. Often, this is due to both known unknowns (the factors that you are considering with imperfect or no information) and unknown unknowns (factors so unexpected that you don't even consider them). You can discover unknown unknowns by involving the perspectives of other people within your organization, consulting external experts and peers at other organizations, and challenging your assumptions when documenting your decision-making criteria and known unknowns.

Another risk is unexpected substitutes, or when people address a problem or need with an unanticipated solution, often from a different industry or unexpected competitor. Online home rentals and streaming video services are famous examples of unexpected substitutes or disruptions from outside the traditional boundaries of an industry. To help you and your team see new possibilities, look at decisions and opportunities through a lens of "How might a startup or new organization without any of our history and limitations approach this problem? If we were starting over, knowing what we do now, what would we do?"

Another risk to decision-making is focusing on what someone says they want or need without understanding why they want or need it. Focusing on what you and your customers want to accomplish, also known as your desired outcomes, allows you to address real wants and needs rather than the limitations of your current approach.

Leading a decision-making process is often complicated. Here are a few questions to help simplify the process:

- "What do you want to accomplish?" keeps the conversation focused on your desired outcome. Your desired outcome is different from the solutions you are considering. Many decision-making processes immediately leap to the solution space and don't spend sufficient time in the problem space. This means many people involved in the decision don't understand what the goal of the decision or what the problem to be solved really is. You want to invite debate to ensure you are solving the right problem and understand what you want to accomplish. A useful framework for understanding what you want to accomplish is "increase/decrease (outcome) as measured by (metric or metrics)," as popularized by Anthony Ulwick.

- "Why?" adds context and purpose to what you want to accomplish. Describing what you want to accomplish and why can open up your decision-making to more data, insight, and critique. I think of this as zooming out. For example, look for opportunities to improve the efficiency of your overall sales and marketing spend versus focusing on a single underperforming channel. This can help you and your team stay open to possibilities that might be excluded with a zoomed-in approach.

- "Whose decision is this?" provides clear decision-making roles and helps decisions keep moving forward. You can improve the way decisions are made on your team if you have a clear, single decision-maker who is informed by other people instead of a committee. If more than one person must be involved in the decision, make the voting process unambiguous.

- "What's the context around the decision?" provides relevant information, including available resources, timelines, and stakeholder details. For example, the size of the team you have to work on the problem might be fixed. You might have a deadline like an upcoming customer meeting. Ensure that everyone involved in the decision has as much context as you can provide.

- "What are our decision-making criteria?" can introduce transparency, consistency, and perceived fairness into your decision-making process. When I was a product leader, people would often say to me, "I wish you could just build what I want," and I would reply with a smile, "I wish I could just build what I want!" Our decision-making criteria for what we built aligned with what our customers wanted to accomplish and our organization's strategy. My own personal desires had nothing to do with it. We held a twice-monthly meeting where we openly shared what we were considering for our roadmap and go-to-market activities. We included ratings and data related to each decision-making criterion. This helped us make better decisions and helped our stakeholders make stronger cases for what they wanted. For example, our head of information security started quantifying the risks associated with his infosec-related requests. Instead of talking generally about what might happen, he gave much-appreciated estimates for the likelihood, severity, and associated costs for each risk. This helped us compare his requests against requests related to increasing revenue and reducing customer churn. Most managers and leaders don't share decision-making criteria, so people have no idea why decisions are made. Assign appropriate weights to the criteria to align with your organization's strategy.

- "How can we introduce data and fresh perspectives into this decision?" keeps you out of what innovator Tom Chi, one of the creators of Google Glass, calls "conjecture land." Most decisions are made based on debates in meetings rather than stakeholder data. You can make significant improvements to your decision-making processes just by creating ways to test your decisions quickly and at a low cost. This might mean making a simple paper prototype that you share with your customers or a whiteboard process diagram that you walk an internal stakeholder through. It doesn't have to be fancy or polished. In fact, simple prototypes help people understand that you want their feedback on something that's in progress. Finding ways to test your decisions can save you a fortune in time and opportunity costs. Introducing fresh perspectives from outside your team can also lead to interesting ideas. When you become an expert, you have such a tremendous wealth of knowledge in your mind that it's nearly impossible to have a beginner's perspective. The solution is inviting fresh perspectives from others into your decision-making process.

- "What might go wrong with each of our options?" stress tests your options and helps you avoid what is sometimes called the "happy path" problem. The happy path involves a mistake-free, perfect plan where everything happens on time and on budget before achieving your desired outcome. Of course, this rarely happens. If you have strengths in hope and optimism (as I do), make sure to ask what can go wrong and involve others who can help you see what might go wrong. This can increase buy-in for your decision as people will feel heard and included. Proactively looking for obstacles—a scientific term for this is "mental contrasting with implementation intentions" from Gabriele Oettingen's research— helps improve your decision and the likelihood of achieving your desired outcome.

As you are moving through your decision-making process, here are some techniques to keep in mind:

1. Separate the problem space and solution space: Make sure you understand the desired outcome, why it's important, and the context before you start solving anything. Many people and teams leap to solving before they understand the problem they are solving.

2. Experimentation versus arguments: Find ways to test your ideas instead of just talking about them. Even brilliant people benefit from gathering data. You can quickly gather data through conversations or by using a paper prototype. Make sure people support their opinions with data and evidence.

3. Decomposition: Breaking decisions and problems into smaller parts can improve and accelerate decision-making. Decomposition also helps you test more quickly with simpler prototypes.

4. Reference class forecasting: Learn from the wins and losses of others. Ask yourself what has happened in previous situations like the one you're in. Talk to others in your field if you can.

5. Outside perspectives: Keep the decision-making team small, but look for ways to find outside perspectives. For example, how might you

involve your stakeholders or customers? Interviewing stakeholders and gathering feedback on low-fidelity prototypes can help you make better decisions. Build a network of peers or mentors at other organizations that you can test decisions on.

6. Look for tailwinds: Look for external trends and new possibilities that you and your team can capitalize on. Look beyond your industry. Similarly, avoid fighting undeniable trends (e.g., Blockbuster and online streaming or Kodak and digital photography, which they invented but feared would destroy their film business).

7. Beginner's mind: Involve people who will see the decision from an informed but fresh perspective. This helps you challenge assumptions and opens up new possibilities.

8. Challenge assumptions: Most decision-making teams don't have a clear understanding of context. Write down your assumptions and invite debate about them.

9. Reason from first principles, not your current situation: Start with a blank page rather than your current state. Start with the fundamentals of business, human behavior, physics, engineering, or your field of expertise.

10. Make your decision-making criteria explicit: Help your people make a better decision by clearly writing down what matters. Assign weights that align with your organization's prioritized goals and strategy. For example, how important is speed to market versus incurring tech debt by building quickly with less testing? How important is revenue growth compared to gross margin?

11. Red team: Consider creating a team to argue against your preferred options using data, evidence, and experimentation. This team can argue for alternatives as well.

Here are some common decision-making pitfalls to avoid:

1. Opinions over experiments: Many teams rely on highly paid guesses decided upon in meetings instead of evidence. Without data, even your most brilliant people are guessing. Gather data from your stakeholders.

2. Lack of clarity about what you want to accomplish: Vague problem statements and goals create bad solutions. Spend time defining what you want to accomplish and why.

3. Unclear decision-making criteria: Many people don't understand what's important to consider. This is

often true even when making million-dollar decisions! Write out and share your decision-making criteria.

4. Accepting assumptions without scrutiny: Our worldviews and perspectives are informed by assumptions. Many assumptions become habitual as we become more expert and experienced. We are often unaware of them. Ask yourself, "Why do I think that way?" and "What do I consider to be common sense about this topic?" Other great reflection questions to reveal assumptions are "What do I believe to be true?" and "What do I know to be true?" Write out your answers to these questions and invite people to challenge them.

5. No decision-making process or timeline: I would bet that 80 percent of decisions are made without either a process or a timeline—or both. Ensure that people understand who is involved and how they are involved. Ensure that people understand the deadline for a decision and why it's a deadline.

6. Involving too many people: Sometimes, managers and leaders consult what seems like dozens or even hundreds of people to make decisions. Diverse perspectives are important. Fresh thinking is important. However, make sure that you are involving people with clear intention and roles.

7. No clear decision-maker: Especially with cross-functional projects, it's often unclear who is responsible for the decision. When no one in particular is responsible, it's easy to come up with excuses such as "we all decided together." Making one person or a small committee responsible for the decision increases accountability.

8. Confirmation bias: Avoid committing to a decision too early. This can unintentionally make you emphasize evidence that supports your decision. Instead, look at evidence objectively. Proactively look for evidence that challenges your decision. Argue the other side.

9. Making decisions that are too big: Many organizations attempt to create strategies that last three years or even five years. They know that their plans only last a few months or, at most, a year! A clear vision and mission empower and inspire your people. An unrealistic amount of detail in your plans makes it hard for people on the front lines of your organization to commit. They know things will change too! Break your decisions into experiments and milestones. Honor the speed of change in today's world.

10. Sunk cost bias: Once you start investing time and money into a program or project, it can be harder to stop it. This is one reason that I suggest you test

ideas using simple prototypes. Instead of a three-month investment in a prototype, test something that took one hour to create. This makes it easier to stop working on the idea or change direction. You can use prototypes for sales and marketing, not just R&D. Quickly create simple scripts and ads to test on your target audience or buyer. Remember that once time and money are spent, they're gone.

11. Choosing a different direction without good reason: Managers and leaders often stay up to date on competitors, external trends, and industry data. While staying informed is valuable, frequently changing direction can demotivate your people. Why should they invest their time, talent, and energy into a strategy that will change in a month? It's important to separate the signal from the noise. Only change direction for compelling reasons. If you do change direction, communicate why, and double-check that everyone understands.

If you follow the guidance above, you will make more informed decisions that you and your people believe in. Once made, decisions should become agreements. Unless you have an escalation process in place for your decision, everyone should commit to the decision as if it was their own. This includes you. Second-guessing decisions in the absence of new information destroys motivation and trust. Be a dynamic follower so others will follow you.

Chapter 8

Collaboration

Collaboration requires excellent communication, valuable meetings, and effective planning. Many managers and organizations struggle with all three of these. However, you can increase the efficiency and engagement of your team through simplicity, focus, and clarity.

Communication

Become a clear, compelling communicator. Work hard on this. If you don't, it will limit your impact, your career, and your ability to realize your vision. Your people want and need honest, authentic, straightforward communication from you. Your people are listening to your words and tone as signals for how they should feel about your organization, their work, and even themselves. Communication between you and your people needs to go both ways, not just from you to your people. Invite feedback as well. We can all learn from the perspectives of others, no matter how senior or experienced we are. There are a number of areas where your communication will significantly impact your people and their performance, safety, and growth.

Communicate in a way that helps your people feel safe, seen, and included. Make trust; don't break trust. Be human, authentic, and transparent. Your people want to work with you, not for you. Invite other people to take the stage with you, deliver important messages, and lead conversations. Remember to be yourself, and be vulnerable.

Communicate what you want to accomplish in a way that's clear and compelling. Your people want and need to be inspired and motivated by your vision and mission. To help your people stay passionate, you need a vision that's so clear that your people can picture it in detail. It should be something you can imagine and immerse yourself in—something you can feel and practically taste, smell, and touch.

Communicate the impact and meaning of your team's work. It's important to regularly tell your people why their work matters and how it positively impacts the world. Whenever possible, invite the people whose lives you've impacted to talk with your people directly.

Communicate what's going well in a way that celebrates and savors progress and wins. Challenge your people to accomplish meaningful goals. When they accomplish them and make progress along the way, make sure your appreciation and recognition are clear.

Communicate what needs to be improved in a way that enables and inspires change. When things don't go well, empathize with your people, and support the necessary changes in a hands-on way. Make sure you communicate why urgent change is needed, how you are going to provide support, and that you believe in the team.

Communicate your decisions and why you made those decisions. Sharing what went into a decision—some might call this showing your work—helps build trust. Remember that people are motivated by knowing why they are doing something. Sharing the why behind the decision can help create buy-in. Also share what's in it for them.

Invite ideas, feedback, and questions, and receive them as a gift no matter how they are delivered. You will sometimes receive important lessons contained in angry, frustrated, and impolite conversations. Don't let the delivery affect the opportunity for growth. Address issues with incivility, hostility, or worse separate from the learning opportunity.

Here are a few practices for improving your communication:

1. Manage what matters. If you have twelve team goals, ten values, and twenty-two key metrics, it's impossible to communicate clearly. Your team

updates will need intermissions! Do less so you and your people can focus.

2. Use written communication whenever it makes sense. Often, people call meetings and share important information in a way that people can't refer back to. When you have something important to say, make sure you write it, even if you also say it. This is especially true for goals, feedback, and agreements.

3. Use grammar and writing tech and tools to check how clear your writing actually is. They aren't perfect, but they are helpful. Many of us, including me, were taught in school that word count matters more than brevity. In the real world, a simpler explanation demonstrates expertise. If you need more help, get a coach.

4. Write like you talk. It may help to use voice-to-text as your first draft. It's easy to rely on jargon and acronyms. Sound like you are speaking.

5. Use short sentences.

6. Manage and lead your people in your own voice, not an inauthentic "leaderly" voice. Don't pretend to be some famous politician or CEO when you address your people. Just talk to them.

7. Tell stories. People remember stories and learn from stories. One of my editors told me that my first draft was clear but read like a dry how-to manual because I hadn't added any stories yet. I want all of you to enjoy reading this book and appreciate the humanity, joy, and fulfillment of people management, so I added that story and others.

8. Be your passionate, hopeful self. You set the tone for your people. Your people need to feel your passion for your team's and your organization's mission. Your people need to know that you believe in your organization. This doesn't mean transforming into an inauthentic, over-the-top version of yourself. It means sharing why your people and their work matter to you and others. Bring obvious positive energy in your own way.

9. Ask for feedback regularly. Ask your people if they understand what's most important. Do they understand why their work matters? How can you better support them and provide the information they need?

10. Repeat what matters. Remind your people regularly what they need to accomplish and why it matters. Don't expect a message to stick after a few repetitions.

In other words, always be honest and authentic as you tell stories, repeat what matters, ask for feedback, answer your team's questions, and support your people's performance, security, and growth.

MEETINGS

Many people, managers and leaders included, hate meetings. Even though the global workforce spends billions of hours in meetings every year, many meetings are inefficient and boring. They are often full of opinions rather than evidence, distraction rather than focused attention, and expectations rather than agreements. You can often dramatically improve the quality of your meetings with a simple agenda and follow-up.

Have a meaningful weekly team meeting. Review your prioritized goals and progress that has been made toward achieving them. Have individuals share how they have fulfilled their agreements related to your goals and leading indicators of whether your goals will be met. Have everyone share something they learned during the previous week. Actively look for ways to support and unblock your people throughout the meeting. Ask questions frequently. Create new agreements that are aligned to your prioritized goals. Keep the tempo of the meeting fast-paced, and involve everyone on your team each week.

Only meet for good reasons. For example, you could meet to facilitate cross-functional collaboration or talk about what's going well and what can be improved with your team. One-on-one meetings with your team members where you connect, prioritize, coach, and provide feedback build and strengthen the connections between you and your team members.

When you are thinking about scheduling a meeting, consider why you are meeting, who should attend, how they should prepare, what will happen during the meeting, and how you will follow up on agreements and additional conversations.

First, ask yourself whether a meeting is the right approach for what you need to accomplish or if you should consider other options, such as asynchronous communication and collaboration. Meetings are most valuable when real-time conversation and collaboration are needed. Meetings can also facilitate human connection and community.

If you decide that a meeting is appropriate, consider your invitees carefully. Only invite people with important roles to play in the meeting. You can invite others who might be interested as optional. If you aren't sure whether someone should attend, explain the purpose of the meeting, and ask them if they want to attend.

Make sure to schedule the right amount of time for your meetings. Just because your calendar software defaults to sixty minutes doesn't mean your meeting shouldn't be ten or fifteen minutes long instead. I like twenty- and fifty-minute meetings rather than thirty or sixty. A shorter time focuses the conversation more quickly and gives a little extra time if we need it.

If you need to schedule a session longer than ninety minutes, include time in your agenda for a short break, or consider multiple meetings instead of one marathon session.

Make the purpose of the meeting clear to everyone you invite. Even at great organizations, many meeting invites lack context, an agenda, and a clear purpose. We've all been invited to a meeting called "Status Update" or "Brainstorming" with no additional information. Give the meeting a descriptive title, and share an agenda and any relevant information and prework with all participants. Err on the side of providing too much information. Because many meetings are poorly run and involve just showing up to talk, you may have to remind people about prework and reviewing materials in advance.

The agenda should explain what will happen during the meeting. If you aim to make a decision during the meeting, ensure you share the right information before the meeting. Confirm that all of the right stakeholders are attending the meeting. I would bet that you've been invited to a decision-making meeting where someone realizes that an important stakeholder is missing after thirty minutes of discussion. This means another repeat meeting. You can help your people and organization by maximizing the value of meetings with proper preparation. Double-check your invitee and accepted lists.

At the beginning of the meeting, take a minute to restate the goal and the agenda and ask if people have any questions. Depending on the meeting and your organization, you may want to ask people to focus their full attention on the meeting.

Even with virtual meetings and video conferences, it's obvious when someone isn't paying attention. You can see people typing and checking their notifications, phone, and watch. If you sent prework, spend time quickly reviewing any prework and ground rules.

During the meeting, ensure that you invite contributions from your key stakeholders. Many valuable contributions go unsaid because meetings are dominated by one or two voices. Especially when some attendees are in person and others are remote, ensure that you specifically invite contributions from everyone. For example, you could ask, "Anything to add?" directed at a specific person. Some people only feel comfortable once they've had a chance to prepare, which is another reason agendas, clear goals, and prework are critical.

Watch out for conjectures, or opinions that are supported by anecdotes rather than data and evidence. Many meetings are filled with opinions, not insights. Saying something like, "That sounds right. What data do you have to support that?" or "That sounds interesting. How might we test that by gathering data?" requests more data without accusing someone of being incorrect. Intuition is important and valuable, and confirming intuition with rapid experimentation can take your team farther faster with less risk.

Sometimes a request for data will be met with defensiveness. For example, the person might respond, "Well, I am responsible for our product marketing, so you would think I know what our customers want." This is an opportunity to demonstrate humility and curiosity. You could say something like, "I appreciate what you are sharing and your expertise, but I need to understand what's supporting your perspective so we can make the right decision and I can share our thinking with my people."

A meeting can also be derailed by a filibuster, which is a long speech by a single person that defeats the purpose of gathering people together to hear multiple perspectives. If you were looking for one person's perspective, you could have asked them to write a report or prepare a presentation instead. I recognize filibusters because I am not afraid of sharing my opinions in meetings, even if the purpose is just getting the conversation going. A favorite line of mine is "This may be a stupid idea, but..." in an attempt to get others thinking differently and talking.

If you see a filibuster in progress, it's simple to say something like, "Wow, you've given us a lot to think about. Thank you! Let's hear what others think." Some meeting software gives you the ability to see who speaks and doesn't speak in meetings. You can coach your people on how to contribute properly with data to support your guidance.

Make sure to watch out for off-topic statements or questions that can derail a meeting. Many meetings are full of tangents because most people are attempting to multitask during the meeting. Unlike improv and brainstorming meetings, where you beautifully "Yes and..." wherever others want the conversation to go, you need a meeting to achieve its purpose. I recommend asking the person to explain how a potential tangent is related to the conversation before you dismiss their thought. You could say, "Thanks for sharing that! Could you share more about how it relates to (meeting goal)?" If there's not a strong connection, a go-to statement that I use is "Thanks for sharing more! It sounds important but not related to the goal of this meeting. I'll add following up on this to our list of possible action items."

It's important to openly value different perspectives, ideas, and worldviews. If you need to move the conversation away from a conjecture, filibuster, or tangent, do it with compassion and candor. Thank the person for sharing their perspective before moving along. If there's an issue where someone needs feedback beyond that, share it in private after the meeting.

When you are planning your agenda, ensure that you have time to create agreements at the end of the meeting. Losing continuity and follow-up between meetings is a waste of time for you and your people. I find it helpful to write or type the agreements so people can see them, and I share them again immediately following the meeting.

After you've shared action items, consider requesting feedback about the quality of the meeting. A simple note asking what went well and what can be improved can demonstrate humility and a desire to better support your colleagues and team. Often, you will receive feedback that reveals blind spots.

PLANNING

Planning is the process of documenting the agreements needed to achieve a desired outcome. Planning is often either an unsophisticated mess or a complicated, acronym-filled monster. As you manage what matters, balance flexibility and speed with efficiency and effectiveness.

Before you start planning, prioritize the right goals and desired outcomes. Once a program or project reaches the size where you are formally planning, you are investing hundreds or thousands of hours of effort. Time is money. Ensure that you, your team, and your organization are investing that time and money effectively. Once you've prioritized the right desired outcomes and goals, planning can begin.

In many organizations, cross-functional programs and projects involve hundreds of stakeholders. I once worked somewhere that invited over a hundred people to review initial proposals for software development projects. This was over 25 percent of our entire organization at the time! When you are planning, balance keeping stakeholders informed with keeping the team as small as possible. Clear communication about your desired outcomes helps people quickly understand how involved they should be.

There are at least a dozen planning and project management frameworks, sometimes called responsibility assignment matrices. These frameworks help document agreements, dependencies, milestones, and more.

In summary, projects consist of milestones, deliverables, and agreements, completed by people in roles to achieve desired outcomes.

Roles

The framework I have found most effective for determining roles is called a RACI matrix.

RACI refers to the roles that people have on specific deliverables within a project:

- **R** = Responsible: those who do the task

- **A** = Accountable: the *one* person ultimately responsible for the completion of the task

- **C** = Consulted: those whose opinions are sought

- **I** = Informed: those who are kept up to date

The same person can have multiple roles. For example, one person may be responsible and accountable for a particular deliverable.

I cannot emphasize the value of checklists enough. I believe in checklists so much that my dissertation was actually about checklists. For cross-functional efforts such as a product or program launch, checklists help you avoid missteps. It's easy to forget about dependencies on other teams or important sign-off processes such as legal or security approvals. A go-to-market checklist within a one-thousand-person organization may include two hundred steps and one hundred stakeholders who need to be involved. Changing your billing system will require dozens if not hundreds of coordinated action items. This is more than anyone can or should attempt to keep in their head or spread across many documents. Checklists are a must for planning and project management.

Speaking of checklists, let's create a checklist for your project plan:

1. Start with the desired outcome that has been properly prioritized. This should be measurable and unambiguous so you can ensure that your people are working on what matters. For example, maybe you want to increase or decrease X as measured by Y.

2. Explain why the desired outcome matters to your organization. Reasons inspire, motivate, and galvanize. Reasons add meaning, and meaning makes the effort worthwhile.

3. Determine who the owner of the project plan is. When people have questions, this will help them find the right person to answer those questions.

4. Document the end date. Specify whether the end date is a date or a deadline. I much prefer

deadlines aligned with public events and agreements, such as an industry conference or customer commitment. Dates have a tendency to "slip," "get pushed," "slide right," and a number of phrases that mean delayed. Deadlines motivate people, as long as it's possible to complete the project by the deadline. Note that possible doesn't mean simple or easy. It just means possible given the context, people, and resources.

5. Include relevant context, such as a list of risks, a living FAQ, and a description of what's out of scope for the project. Before the project kickoff, talk with your team about what might go wrong, and create plans for avoiding the most impactful budget, people, and technical risks. Answering questions in one place helps people stay informed and reduces the burden on whoever is managing the project, and documenting what's out of scope early avoids the natural inclination for projects to grow.

6. Create clear, explicit descriptions of what's expected for each deliverable. Err on the side of too much detail, especially when collaborating cross-functionally and with new team members. Words mean different things at different organizations and across different teams in the same organization. Double-check that everyone has clarity on accountabilities and agreements.

7. Document the roles for each deliverable, including who is responsible, accountable, consulted, and informed.

8. Include clear, explicit descriptions of who will do what by when, organized by deliverable.

9. Schedule appropriate milestones when desired outcomes or specific deliverables are completed. Similar to deadlines, milestones should be meaningful, such as previewing the project deliverable with your executive team or scheduling meetings with early adopters. Nonspecific milestones like "this quarter" will most likely be delayed.

10. Schedule meetings every week or two to discuss progress, obstacles, what's going well, what can be improved, and any adjustments to the plan. Regular meetings help identify issues early, but make sure to keep the meetings short and purposeful and cancel if there's nothing to cover during a particular week. You can also provide status updates asynchronously.

Remember to keep your project planning and project management simple. Effective project management can be done in a shared document or spreadsheet, especially for a small team, but you may consider purchasing project management software if your projects involve dependencies and cross-functional collaboration. While project management software is inexpensive, the costs associated with learning how to use the software are much higher. Ideally, your project management software will integrate with other tools that you use. Otherwise, the project manager may be the only person using the software, defeating its purpose.

CONTINUOUS LEARNING AND IMPROVEMENT

Winning teams and organizations learn and improve quickly. High-performing people crave feedback, growth, and learning. Ask yourself and others, "What's going well?" and "What can be improved?" regularly and frequently. Have meetings and ceremonies, such as retrospectives and one-on-ones, to proactively solicit feedback, and make sure you are learning on a daily and weekly cadence, not a quarterly or annual cycle. Create metrics and key results related to your prioritized goals that allow you and your people to understand where you are on and off track. There are many frameworks, tools, and certifications associated with continuous improvement, such as kaizen and lean.

Here are a few recommendations for improving continuously while keeping things simple:

- Rely on actuals, not conjectures. Tom Chi put into words something I have been practicing for twenty years: rely on actuals, not conjectures. Actuals are people responding directly to prototypes and products. Conjectures are smart people arguing in meetings. Gather feedback from the real people you and your team serve. You can get actuals using paper prototypes, whiteboard line drawings, and simple sales scripts. Prototypes don't have to be fancy or expensive.

- Be curious, not defensive. Once you start gathering feedback, you may find yourself defending your decisions with explanations and excuses. Learn by asking questions instead, even if you think you've heard it all before. Many of the best conversations I've ever had about improving something I've been working on started with ten minutes of "things I already knew." As the conversations continued, new perspectives and opportunities to learn appeared. Honor the person delivering the feedback with your attention and curiosity.

- Involve your team in the learning and improving process through retrospectives, debriefs, one-on-ones, and reviews. Meet every two to four weeks to talk about what's going well and what can be improved, and then take immediate action on the improvements with the best return on investment. Spread accountability and ownership of the improvements across your team. Do the same during individual one-on-ones, and remember to zoom out and take a broader perspective as well.

- Enable anonymous and confidential feedback. Importantly, not everyone at your organization will always feel comfortable sharing their honest opinion and concerns on every topic. Provide people with an anonymous, confidential way to share feedback. This helps surface critical opportunities and minimize blind spots.

Remember that almost all feedback is data, not a directive. Look for themes and opportunities that are impactful, aligned with your values, and worth the investment required. Remember that trying to do everything or please everyone practically guarantees failure.

As you are gathering data and feedback to learn and improve, continue to manage what matters: performance, security, and growth. Sometimes managers and leaders can become reactive and distracted. Don't lose sight of what's most important.

CONFLICT RESOLUTION

Conflict is inevitable. Most conflict is good and leads to resolution and growth, but some is poisonous and ruins relationships, reducing the likelihood of success. Some conflict can only be resolved by involving your people/HR team and your legal team.

You can minimize the risk of conflict through the following values and practices:

- Compassionate candor: Deliver the truth with kindness.

- Agreements, not expectations: Get clear on who will do what by when. Don't assume.

- Aim to uplift: Share feedback with the intention of uplifting yourself and others.

- Share feedback in real time: Don't let small issues grow into problems.

- No triangles, no gossip: Get coaching and support when you need it, but share feedback directly with the other person.

- Observations, not advice: Share what you saw, heard, and noticed, not how you think it should be fixed.

Remember that we are all works in progress. Don't expect others to be perfect.

When conflict arises, work to resolve it. Fortunately, the same framework for sharing observations works when resolving conflicts. Have a conversation focused on understanding and agreements, built on safety and mutual respect.

All managers and leaders should familiarize themselves with the fundamentals of nonviolent communication. The Center for Nonviolent Communication is a global nonprofit organization founded by Marshall Rosenberg, PhD. Nonviolent communication involves communicating from a natural state of compassion and concern for others, without judgment or blame. The steps involved in nonviolent communication include making observations rather than evaluations, revealing your feelings, not your opinions, communicating your needs instead of criticism, and making requests, not demands.

Often, conflict occurs because of expectations instead of agreements. The two people involved have different understandings of the relationship or who will do what by when. Ensure that clear agreements exist to avoid future conflicts.

Sometimes, resolving conflict requires a third party. If you are involved as a mediator, focus on listening and understanding with compassion and empathy. Use the observations guide, and ensure that you give both parties an opportunity to share observations. Encourage the parties to talk directly to each other rather than to you. Reflect back what you are hearing to create clarity and help people find common ground and shared respect. Facilitate agreements about who will do what by when.

PART 3

BECOMING A MEANINGFUL MANAGER

You've learned about what matters, as well as the fundamentals and practices required for becoming a meaningful manager. I hope that you have successfully applied some or all of the practices as you've been learning about becoming a meaningful manager. Combining what you've learned into a simple, powerful system will allow you to maximize your positive impact on your team and organization without requiring sixteen-hour workdays or around-the-clock availability. Let's get started!

CHAPTER 9

CREATING YOUR OWN MEANINGFUL MANAGEMENT SYSTEM

A well-designed meaningful management system involves a coherent combination of technology, tools, and feedback loops. Let's review the building blocks so you can create your own meaningful management system.

- To be a meaningful manager, manage what matters.

- Managing what matters starts with your meaning, passions, strengths, values, and vision.

- Three things matter: performance, security, and growth.

- Five practices help you: prioritized goals, feedback, one-on-ones, decision-making, and collaboration.

- Three fundamentals support you: presence, empathy, and agreements.

- Managing what matters is simple and scalable but often not easy.

- You are a work in progress on your journey to increasing and reaching your highest potential.

- You're a masterpiece who can make a significant impact right now as you learn and grow.

As you are creating your approach, remember that you matter. Sometimes, managers and leaders forget to take care of themselves because they are busy achieving business outcomes and supporting their teams. This can work for a little while, but it's a losing long-term approach. Taking care of yourself helps you support your team as well. Your management system should include self-care, healthy selfishness, and self-compassion.

- Self-care involves properly prioritizing your own physical, mental, and spiritual health, including your sleep, rest, renewal, hydration, nutrition, and exercise. Consult the right experts—physicians, psychiatrists, therapists, nutritionists, personal trainers, mindfulness experts, etc.—and schedule time on your calendar focused on you, your body, your mind, and your spirit. Treat time focused on your health and well-being the way you would a meeting with your most important client—rarely canceled and always rescheduled.

- Healthy selfishness is about reminding yourself that you matter and ensuring that you invest the right amount of time and energy into your needs. Many of us, myself included, are better at serving and caring for others than ourselves. Healthy selfishness is about balancing your own needs with the needs of others and having healthy boundaries. Healthy selfishness gives you permission to invest appropriately in self-care, even when you have other responsibilities.

- Self-compassion is about being there for yourself in times of need. During tough times, be kind to yourself the way you would be kind to a dear friend. Many of us don't treat ourselves like good friends in times of need. A great reflection to ask yourself during a tough time may be "How would I treat my best friend if they were going through this situation?" How would you treat someone you love? Many of us blame and criticize ourselves in ways that are quite different than how we would treat someone we love. As managers and leaders, we're in situations where we win and situations where we lose. When we lose or experience a setback, we need to feel and acknowledge our emotions as we learn from the experience.

It's also important to take vacations and time away from work. In today's always-on workplaces, managers and leaders often start working upon awakening by checking their phones, and then, after a day of meetings, decisions, and task switching, they check their email and notifications before they fall asleep. You need time away from work to recharge and renew. Stepping away from work often leads to new ideas and inspiration as well. Burnout is insidious. Be a good example for your team, and take care of yourself in visible ways.

Ensure that your management system allows for frequent vacations and time off. Create redundancies so that you and your people can spend time away from work. The work will be there when you return. While you're off, stay away from your phone and other reminders of work. Too many people's idea of vacation is lying on the beach or hiking through the woods while answering emails and checking in. Demonstrate trust by giving people opportunities to make decisions and keep things moving in your absence. This helps them grow—and helps you grow.

YEAR IN THE LIFE

With the right management system, you can have an exceptional impact on your organization and your people each year. Creating a management system requires new habits and practices. Here's a simple MESSY framework for creating new habits because, well, change is MESSY:

- Matters: Align your new habits to something that genuinely matters to you.

- Energizes: Choose tactics that energize you. Be your best self, not an imitation of someone else.

- Simple: Make it as simple as possible.

- Schedule it: Remind yourself by scheduling time for it. If something isn't scheduled, it rarely happens.

- Y (Why): Regularly remind yourself why the change matters.

One of the best and simplest ways to accelerate change is by adding things to your calendar. Schedule time for your own work, and defend it.

A year in the life of a manager should include the following:

- Create a three-year vision that includes meaning, passions, strengths, and values. Review and update this vision at least every month.

- Create prioritized professional and personal goals at least once per year, and review and update them at least once per month.

- Review your progress toward your professional and personal goals and your team's goals at least once per month.

- Schedule one-on-one meetings with each of your people and with your manager at least every two weeks. Hold team-level retrospectives at least once per month and team-building events at least once every three months.

- Conduct confidential surveys and have individual review conversations focused on performance, security, and growth at least every six months. Schedule at least one meeting with each of your people focused on their vision, meaning, passions, strengths, and values each year.

- Have at least one meeting-less day each month for deep work and getting things done (e.g., strategic planning, agreement audits, expenses, administrative work).

- Conduct at least one meeting audit each quarter and one agreement audit each month.

- Take at least one vacation (even a three- or four-day weekend) every quarter where you completely disconnect from your work.

- Schedule at least one transformative experience each year, focused on elevating your own performance, security, and growth.

These practices will help you manage what matters and will positively influence your team, your organization, and even yourself.

WEEK IN THE LIFE

Sprints—a practice that breaks work into increments of a few weeks—are one of my favorite practices. Sprints allow for progress to be reviewed and celebrated regularly, priorities to be adjusted before work is wasted, and work to be shipped frequently. Thinking of each week as a sprint for your management system can help elevate your performance, increase security, and accelerate growth.

Each week, do the following:

- Read your three-year vision.

- Review your own, your team's, and your organization's prioritized goals, and make sure you're making progress on them.

- Review your agreements and reagree as needed. Fulfill all agreements for the week.

- Review your calendar for the week, and update plans as necessary.

- Take uninterrupted time for deep work.

- Share recognition, encouragement, observations, advice, and redirection with each of your people. Remember to include at least one reminder to your team about why their work matters and why they matter.

- Proactively reach out to your team, asking, "How can I best support you right now?"

- Lead your up-tempo team meeting that focuses on reviewing prioritized goals, recognizing progress, including everyone, unblocking people, and creating new agreements.

You can make time for these practices by scheduling a one-hour one-on-one with yourself each week.

DAY IN THE LIFE

Set the standard for your team by making meaningful progress on meaningful work each day. Given the demands of meetings, updates, and coordination, it's easy for managers and leaders to let days and weeks slip by with minimal impact. Create a management system that allows you to seize each day.

- Establish the three things you will accomplish each day. You can do almost anything, but not everything.

- Review and update your calendar. Find the balance between collaboration and deep work.

- Fulfill any agreements for the day.

- Do something that restores you.

- Do something that energizes you.

- Check in with yourself on your physical, mental, and spiritual well-being.

Establishing a new management system may take a few weeks or even months, but you can start immediately with one new practice and then add another and another. Your success and fulfillment depend on it.

As you create your management system, remember that humans appreciate variety as well. Systems and processes facilitate success. However, many humans are bored and unmotivated without variety and new challenges. Here are some ways you can introduce variety and interest to your approach:

- Share a powerful shift or movement in the world that you are leading or participating in.

- Disclose a new challenge or reframe an old one.

- Meet directly with the stakeholders that you serve.

- Celebrate the end of your current chapter and the start of a new one. Any day can be a fresh start!

- Have a new experience together—attend a conference, meet with a senior leader, complete a course.

- Have everyone on the team do someone else's role for a week.

- Twenty percent time—for three months, give everyone one day a week to work on a passion project.

- One-week innovation sprint—allow everyone to work on something new and experimental for a week.

- Surprise your team with a day off or self-care day after an intense period—or just because we all need rest and renewal. One of my team leads used to tell me to go count the doorknobs in my house—corny, but I always appreciated a surprise day off!

Chapter 10

Your Next Level

Learning and Growing as a Leader

Congratulations! You've created a simple, powerful system for becoming a meaningful manager and increasing performance, security, and growth. Take a moment to recognize the agreement you are making with yourself to be a meaningful manager and leader—not just a supervisor, not just an approver of vacation time, not just a once-per-year reviewer of performance, but someone who will help their people perform, feel safe, and grow. That clear intention and the system you've created have already differentiated you from many other managers and leaders.

So, what's next?

First, consider reviewing your vision statement. Find a different perspective to review it from. You can even find a new physical vantage point, such as sitting in your normal chair in your normal workplace but facing in a new direction. Go to a park if you can. Print it out, and read it aloud.

- Does it still resonate?

- Does it still reflect what you want?

- Does it still inspire you?

- Have your values shifted?

- Are you dreaming bigger now that you have more skills and tools?

Take a little time and look deeply at yourself. You matter, and you deserve a life worth living. Once you've reviewed and updated your vision statement, ask yourself how you would like to grow next. This requires self-awareness informed by the feedback you've received. Do you want to further develop a strength? Add a new skill? Learn more about business? Find ways to connect with your people? Improve your persuasion skills? Develop a new habit to help address a blind spot or weakness? You can do almost anything, but you can't do everything.

Get specific about how you want to grow and why.

After you reflect on your vision statement and how you would like to grow, think about who can guide, support, and help you. Think broadly about communities, books, courses, podcasts, tech, apps, and videos, in addition to people that you know. Also, reach out and ask me! I love learning and supporting people like you as you increase and reach your highest potential.

You can also learn and grow by making. Passively reading books or listening to podcasts can be enjoyable and educational, but I've found that accelerated growth and transformation come from actively engaging with what you are reading, watching, and listening to. Take notes and build your own models and approaches. Bruce Lee famously pulled from different disciplines and martial arts when he created the martial art of Jeet Kune Do. My therapist does this as she learns about different practices and approaches. Use *The Meaningful Manager* as your foundation, but do the same. Take what works from different sources, and combine them into your own vision statement, management system, and approach to growth and transformation.

This might seem counterintuitive, but your fastest path to growth might be doing less. Many managers and leaders are overwhelmed by meetings, agreements, their own goals, people issues, and more. Regularly review how you are spending your time and energy, and look for things you can remove from your calendar or stop doing. I once conducted a workshop where we reviewed the roles and responsibilities of the product managers on our team. We created a list of over eighty independent things we were responsible for! How could anyone be successful with eighty different accountabilities? Our path to increasing performance and well-being was through subtraction and focus. Yours may be as well. Prioritized goals, one-on-ones, and feedback are a simple, winning combination for people management.

Learn and grow for a clear reason. Habit change, growth, learning, and transformation are messy and difficult. Align the changes you want to make to something that truly matters to you. Change rarely happens without a compelling reason.

Self-development goals are another way to continue your growth. If you do set a self-development goal, make sure you prioritize it and define it the same way that you would a performance-related goal. Too many self-development goals are ambiguous, saying things like "Learn about our business." A properly defined self-development goal for a quarter might read, "Read three books about strategy. Have someone from our finance team walk our team through our P&L and balance sheet. Earn an online certification from a top business school."

ONGOING GROWTH: RECEIVING FEEDBACK AS A GIFT, EVEN WHEN IT'S NOT DELIVERED LIKE ONE

Feedback enables ongoing growth. Proactively request feedback regularly. "What's going well?" "What can be improved?" and "How can I best support you right now?" should basically become your taglines as a manager and leader. Taking action on the answers to these questions will immediately take your management and leadership to another level.

Sometimes feedback will not be delivered like a gift. The most valuable and important feedback is often filled with negative emotions like frustration and anger. You might be surprised and blindsided by it. You might feel betrayal. You might wish the person had talked to you about the feedback weeks or months ago.

As an executive coach, I sometimes did 360 feedback debriefs with people I had previously never met. I would receive an envelope with their results as they walked into a room. All of these people were VP or C-level. Sometimes, the feedback was callous and hurtful enough that it would make them cry, even in the presence of a stranger. I would attempt to feel with them. Their most common reaction was betrayal, a feeling of "Why didn't they tell me before?"

This emphasizes the importance of sharing feedback even when it's hard. In fact, receiving, considering, and learning from all feedback is such a powerful skill that I call it a superpower or super strength. The most memorable feedback I ever received is that I sound bored on my own webinars. Bored by my own webinars! Worse, he was right! Fortunately, I was too surprised by the feedback to offer an explanation or excuse, so the conversation continued. We realized that I needed to adopt the mentality of a performing artist for my audience. I needed to bring energy, even if I had presented the information dozens of times before. This feedback and learning literally changed the trajectory of my career. (Thanks, Bob!)

Here are some things to remember about feedback to help you receive it as a gift:

- Your feelings are valid. If you are frustrated, angered, or upset by the feedback, make time to fully explore and process those emotions. This happens to everyone.

- Feedback is data. Some of it is meaningful and helpful. Some of it says more about the person giving it than it does about you. I recommend listening to and considering all feedback but not following all feedback. When you reframe feedback as data, you can think of yourself as a scientist conducting research about yourself.

- Demonstrate appreciation and curiosity. For example, you could say, "Thanks for sharing that with me. It takes courage to share something like that with someone. It seems like this is important to you. Would you please share more details with me?" Don't attempt to defend yourself with an excuse or explanation or one-up them with negative feedback about them. Just ask questions and listen.

- Ensure they feel heard and valued. Repeat what you heard. According to Chris Voss, it's a good sign if they say, "That's right," when you share what you heard.

- Thank the person again, and say you'll reflect on what they shared with you. Don't feel an obligation to agree to anything or say that you'll change. Schedule a follow-up conversation if needed.

Note that I am specifically not suggesting that you tolerate anything resembling abuse, a hostile work environment, or harassment of any kind. If you encounter any of these things, follow your organization's policies immediately. Involve outside counsel if necessary. You deserve to feel safe and secure.

REVIEWS AS AN OPPORTUNITY FOR GROWTH

Even with a couple of annoying "forced ranking" stories behind me, I strangely look forward to performance reviews. Maybe it's because I've bought into this "feedback is data" concept, or maybe it's my experience as a UX researcher and product leader constantly searching for feedback. I am fortunate to have had supportive managers throughout my career, so I suspect my experience with reviews is unusual. Most reviews involve a quick summary of accomplishments followed by a few imprecise statements about shortcomings. Here are a few tactics for increasing the value of the reviews that you receive:

- Explain why you are looking forward to the review process. Your manager may think you are expecting another throwaway experience. Make it clear that you are looking for specific feedback about what's going well and what can be improved.

- Come prepared. With your vision statement in mind, you know what you want to achieve. Be explicit about what you need from your manager to achieve your vision.

- Ask clarifying questions. If feedback is vague, ask for more detail. Many people lack self-awareness, so your manager may think they are giving wonderfully useful feedback even if you don't think so.

- Remember that your manager may not have good advice for you on how to resolve an issue. Sometimes people can describe a problem but not a solution. This is why "Don't bring me problems unless you have solutions" is an example of awful management. Follow up with a plan for improving yourself, and ask for the resources to do so. For example, you could join an online community for managers and leaders. Dive deeply into your self-awareness to enable your self-actualization.

- Ask, "What's something I could take ownership of that would free up your time?" Explicitly show your manager that you are looking for more if you are.

Reviews are an opportunity to talk about and learn from both wins and losses. Many people attempt to learn from losses. Some people celebrate and savor wins. Almost no one learns from wins. Examining the reasons behind success should be part of your performance reviews. Fortunately, you can do this on your own with or without the support of your manager. Give yourself time and space to think deeply about a time when you felt powerful, energized, and successful. Ask yourself the following questions:

- Which of your strengths did you use the most?

- What made you feel powerful?

- What motivated you about this effort?

- When did you feel most energized?

- Who helped you?

- How did they enable your success?

- Who did your work impact?

- How did it help them?

- What obstacles surfaced?

- How did you overcome those obstacles?

- What about the situation helped you be successful?

- How well was the work aligned with your values, strengths, and motivations?

- How much clarity did you have about the desired outcome?

- How much autonomy were you given?

- How much feedback were you given?

- How much recognition were you given?

Use what you noticed about your specific success story to craft future success when you are planning an initiative.

Savor wins. Learn from them. Avoiding what you think made you fail is only part of the equation for success. Understand what's working as well.

Conclusion

Congratulations! You've reached the end of *The Meaningful Manager*! I sincerely hope you feel seen, supported, and inspired. As a manager and leader, you can and will make a meaningful impact on your people. Whether that impact is positive or negative is up to you.

Remember that we are masterpieces and works in progress! We are all learning and growing together. Start with one new practice, and then add another and another.

Being present with your people, listening empathetically, and upholding your agreements will have a dramatic impact on you and your people. Adding prioritized goals helps your people understand where to focus their energy and why. One-on-ones allow you to give your people the recognition, encouragement, observations, and coaching they want and deserve. Better decisions and collaboration motivate and inspire those around you.

Creating a management system that works for you at your organization will increase your positive impact without requiring that you work around the clock or read every business book ever written. You have everything you need within this book to become a meaningful manager.

Please connect with me at jeffsmithphd.com and on LinkedIn @jeffsmithphd for more on management and leadership. As you can imagine, I would love to hear your feedback!

Thanks for learning with me! I hope to connect with you soon.

Appendix I

How to Increase Meaningful Management across Your Organization

In my experience, managers do not have the impact that they could and should in most organizations. Your managers should be elevating the performance, security, and growth of your team members substantially. From a simple financial perspective, your managers should be creating value at least to match what you invest in them. This breaks even on your investment (if they exceed the cost of capital). Otherwise, your organization might be better off without managers!

Does every manager in your organization make a meaningful impact and create the level of value that they need to? Unfortunately, this is unlikely. Are any of your managers having a negative impact on the performance, security, and growth of their people and your organization? In other words, would any of your people be better off without their manager? I hope not.

Here are a few of the common problems in many organizations and solutions that could help managers be as impactful as possible:

PROBLEM: Lack of clear expectations. If you ask one hundred managers what it means to be a manager, you will receive one hundred different answers. Very few organizations define what it means to be a manager or leader within their organization, and many blend playing and coaching. Since many managers only have one or two direct reports, they need to make a substantial impact as individual contributors as well.

SOLUTION: Create clear agreements for what it means to be a manager in your organization. Keep it simple—performance, security, and growth. Ensure that people understand what's required before they apply to be a manager, and have simple policies for them to follow. Resist the urge to have twenty-five management and leadership competencies. The 80/20 rule applies. Create agreements based on desired outcomes that allow freedom and flexibility. Make sure there are clear differences across titles like manager, senior manager, director, VP, and so on. Ensure consistency in the different departments across your organization. Revise and update your agreements based on your organization's needs. Provide recommended resources for people related to each agreement, such as this book. There are excellent, inexpensive resources for all relevant skills and agreements.

PROBLEM: Lack of measurement. Because expectations for managers are unclear, performance agreements aren't created, and performance isn't managed.

SOLUTION: Measure manager performance against your clear agreements. How are they increasing the impact of their people? How are they impacting your organization?

PROBLEM: Lack of data and feedback. Most managers and leaders receive feedback on their performance only once per year, and the data and feedback aren't always aligned to a clear set of agreements.

SOLUTION: Proactively gather and share feedback about their performance. Just like everyone else, managers are masterpieces and works in progress. Managers need regular feedback on their performance so they can evolve and improve. Comprehensively look at data related to their performance and their team's performance. Use a mix of quality, quantity, complexity, and influence measures as part of your review process.

Managers should proactively search for ways to improve. Help them by using tech and ceremonies where people provide feedback on what's going well and what can be improved. Use engagement surveys and review processes that focus on performance, security, and growth, and ensure people can provide anonymous feedback in case there's a psychological safety issue.

PROBLEM: Lack of accountability. Because manager performance isn't measured, managers aren't held accountable for shortfalls and oversights.

SOLUTION: Hold your managers accountable using your clear agreements and measurements. Sometimes you may need to place a manager on a performance improvement plan because they aren't fulfilling their management duties. For example, managers must be able to hold their people accountable for high performance, and they must actively participate in conflict resolution instead of hiding from conflict.

PROBLEM: Lack of initiative and learning. The last thing that most people want to do is receive a promotion and then admit that they have no idea what it means to manage people.

SOLUTION: Make it okay to ask for help and support. Have your CEO or another senior leader talk with your managers about how no one has all the answers. Make it easy and normal for managers to ask their managers, a peer, or a people/ HR team member for help and support. Give new managers a manager buddy to help bring them up to speed. People management can be hard and lonely, especially as a first-time manager afraid to ask for help.

PROBLEM: Lack of training. Most managers receive little to no training. Even when training is provided, it's often not reinforced, incorporated into their "real work," or aligned against clear agreements for managers.

SOLUTION: Provide a comprehensive manager training program. Make it clear that there are new agreements for people managers. Organizations should have two employee experience calendars: one aligned with the annual calendar and the other aligned to individual start dates. Schedule monthly manager education sessions for all of your managers to reinforce critical, timely topics. Provide additional onboarding experiences for new managers, and onboard internal promotions as if they are new to your organization. Train everyone in your organization (not just managers) on fundamental skills like giving and receiving feedback in an ongoing way.

PROBLEM: Lack of partnerships with people and HR teams. Most managers don't know why, how, and when to partner with people and HR teams.

SOLUTION: Proactively build relationships between your managers and your people/HR team. Make it simple and normal to partner with people and HR teammates. Have people and HR contacts for every manager, and make it obvious which people and HR contacts help with different topics.

PROBLEM: Lack of motivation. Many people only become people managers because it's the only way to be promoted. They don't actually want to manage people, but they want to be a director or VP someday.

SOLUTION: Create a dual-track approach to promotions so people can be promoted to leadership positions without becoming people managers. This keeps people from taking on people management responsibilities they don't actually want just to get the title they want. I worked at IBM for a number of years, and this was something that IBM did exceedingly well. You could be promoted to the equivalent of an SVP without any people management responsibilities. People could go back and forth between management and nonmanagement roles. There were clear agreements for what was necessary to be promoted to an executive role as an individual contributor. It was challenging and not based on tenure in role. Create something similar in your organization. Also, help people understand what it takes to be a meaningful manager before they become one, with a manager preview program.

PROBLEM: Lack of technology. Most organizations default to only training managers rather than providing technology as well.

SOLUTION: Provide your managers with the right technology for people management. Help them create, align, and prioritize goals and have better one-on-ones with their people. Make sure they can gather feedback on what's going well and what can be improved so they can make better decisions. Help them collaborate with their team and across teams. Support them with technology as you ask them to support the performance, security, and growth of their people.

Help managers understand evidence-based best practices for their highest leverage activities. Goals, one-on-ones, feedback, decision-making, and collaboration encompass the vast majority of a manager's impact. Make them comfortable with gathering feedback and continuously improving. Ensure they've mastered these fundamentals, and provide additional education and coaching when they do.

If this sounds like a significant investment, it is. However, you can start with this book, clear manager agreements, and build from there.

Appendix II

Recommended Books and Resources

Successful managers and leaders are constantly learning and growing. Since I am frequently asked for book recommendations for managers and leaders, here are my top books to supplement *The Meaningful Manager: How to Manage What Matters*. I'm a nerd. I read a lot. These are books that I have not only read but also refer back to.

High Output Management by Andrew S. Grove
The rare business book that deserves to be savored because value is shared on every page. It would take another book to summarize all of its wisdom.

Man's Search for Meaning by **Viktor E. Frankl**
A Holocaust survivor and iconoclastic neurologist and psychiatrist not only shares his incredible story of survival through meaning but also reorients humanity's primary drive as the search for meaning and purpose.

Illuminate: Ignite Change Through Speeches, Stories, Ceremonies, and Symbols by **Nancy Duarte and Patti Sanchez**
Clear guidance on how to become a better storyteller and choose the right stories based on where you and your team are and where you are going to inspire your people.

Year of Yes: How to Dance It Out, Stand in the Sun, and Be Your Own Person by **Shonda Rhimes**
An exceptional storyteller shares her own tale about a year of saying yes to every possibility.

Die with Zero: Getting All You Can from Your Money and Your Life by **Bill Perkins**
How to maximize your memorable moments by investing in peak experiences throughout your life and not waiting for retirement.

Rise and Grind: Out-Perform, Out-Work and Out-Hustle Your Way to a More Successful and Rewarding Life by **Daymond John**
A powerful reminder of the impact of sustained, focused effort and energy on what matters most to you.

Grit: The Power of Passion and Perseverance
by **Angela Duckworth**
The science of rising and grinding and how it can lead to top performance.

The Progress Principle: Using Small Wins to Ignite Joy, Engagement, and Creativity at Work by **Teresa Amabile and Steven Kramer**
Seeing and recognizing meaningful progress on meaningful work might be the most cost-effective way to increase performance and growth on your team.

Good Strategy, Bad Strategy by **Richard P. Rumelt**
Breaks the often ambiguous concept of strategy into a practical, simple, coherent framework that helps you avoid common pitfalls related to strategy, such as creating a list of goals and calling them a strategy.

Executive Coaching with Backbone and Heart: A Systems Approach to Engaging Leaders with Their Challenges by **Mary Beth O'Neill**
Reminds us that courage, candor, and compassion are not mutually exclusive and are in fact all required for excellent coaching, leadership, and management.

Positive Leadership: Strategies for Extraordinary Performance by **Kim Cameron**
Infuses leadership guidance and advice with the power of positive psychology and positive organizational scholarship.

No Mud, No Lotus: The Art of Transforming Suffering
by **Thich Nhat Hanh**
A beautiful guide to mindfulness and how being present eases and transforms suffering.

The Advice Trap: Be Humble, Stay Curious & Change the Way You Lead Forever by **Michael Bungay Stanier**
Reminds managers to coach rather than give advice and supports the shift with practical guidance.

Scrum: The Art of Doing Twice the Work in Half the Time by **Jeff Sutherland and J.J. Sutherland**
Fast, readable introduction to how scrum can immediately make your team more organized, efficient, and productive.

Financial Intelligence: A Manager's Guide to Knowing What the Numbers Really Mean by **Karen Berman and Joe Knight, with John Case**
You can't reach your highest potential as a leader unless you understand the language of business. This book introduces the art and science of finance comprehensively but accessibly.

Retrain Your Brain: Cognitive Behavioral Therapy in 7 Weeks: A Workbook for Managing Anxiety and Depression by **Seth J. Gillihan**
Managers shouldn't pretend to be therapists, but caring about your people involves understanding them. This book helps you identify thought patterns and behaviors that aren't working so you can replace them with better ones.

The Gifts of Imperfection: Let Go of Who You Think You're Supposed to Be and Embrace Who You Are by **Brené Brown**
Reminds us that we are all imperfect and capable of living authentic, meaningful, fulfilling, wholehearted lives anyway.

Flourish: A Visionary New Understanding of Happiness and Well-Being by **Martin Seligman**
The father of positive psychology on well-being, positive emotions, engagement, relationships, meaning, and accomplishment.

The Power of Character Strengths: Appreciate and Ignite Your Positive Personality by **Ryan M. Niemiec and Robert E. McGrath**
A guide to how your character strengths can help you increase resilience, reduce stress, and find greater fulfillment.

Daily Rituals: Women at Work by **Mason Currey**
Fascinating short stories about impactful, creative women and their unique approaches to their life's work that remind us there's no one way to live, be successful, or find fulfillment.

Crucial Conversations: Tools for Talking When the Stakes are High by **Joseph Grenny, Kerry Patterson, Ron McMillan, Al Switzler, and Emily Gregory**
The go-to, step-by-step approach for resolving high-stakes, high-emotion conflicts.

Never Split the Difference: Negotiating As If Your Life Depended on It **by Chris Voss, with Tahl Raz**
Fascinating stories, hard-earned wisdom, and practical guidance about communication, negotiation, and psychology from the FBI's former top international kidnapping negotiator.

Nonviolent Communication: Create Your Life, Your Relationships, and Your World in Harmony with Your Values **by Marshall Rosenberg**
A step-by-step process for reducing conflict and tension while honoring our own needs and the needs of others.

The Hard Thing about Hard Things: Building a Business When There Are No Easy Answers **by Ben Horowitz**
Honest, hard-hitting stories about the realities of leadership from an entrepreneur-turned-venture capitalist.

Leading without Authority: How the New Power of Co-Elevation Can Break Down Silos, Transform Teams, and Reinvent Collaboration **by Keith Ferrazzi, with Noel Weyrich**
Inspiring call to go higher together in times of stress by committing to a shared mission and caring about others, not just ourselves.

Transcend: The New Science of Self-Actualization **by Scott Barry Kaufman**
Learn how to reach your highest potential and help others do so as well with what I consider to be the best book on psychology and human needs ever written.

The Fearless Organization: Creating Psychological Safety in the Workplace for Learning, Innovation, and Growth by Amy C. Edmondson
Create safe spaces for your team to talk about what's going well and what can be improved to accelerate learning and growth.

Atomic Habits: An Easy & Proven Way to Build Good Habits & Break Bad Ones by James Clear
Emphasizes the importance of creating systems for habit change rather than just relying on your own willpower.

The Dichotomy of Leadership: Balancing the Challenges of Extreme Ownership to Lead and Win by Jocko Willink and Leif Babin
An excellent follow-up to *Extreme Ownership* that describes the balance between leadership and followership, focusing and zooming out, and being aggressive and prudent.

Orbiting the Giant Hairball: A Corporate Fool's Guide to Surviving with Grace by Gordon MacKenzie
A brilliant rallying cry for creativity to awaken in all of us as we navigate the bureaucracies, rules, and contradictions present in most organizations.

The Checklist Manifesto: How to Get Things Right by Atul Gawande
A great book and more of a mindset for me: if you have a complex problem, the solution can be as simple and inexpensive as a checklist.

Acknowledgments

Thank you to the people I have been honored to manage directly and educate about people management. I have learned so much from the situations we've been through together and the questions that you've asked.

Thank you to my managers throughout my career, including Kim, Paul, Tony, Bryan, Randy, Jennifer, Jenn, Roland, Randy, Doug, Shawn, Tom, Adam, Rebecca, David, and Erik. I am grateful for your support, guidance, and advice. I realize I am not always easy to manage, and I am grateful for your patience.

Thank you to my colleagues, clients, and customers. I am honored to work for and love your success.

Thank you to the researchers and creators whose lives and work continue to inspire me, especially Viktor Frankl. It's an honor to refer others to the exceptional, prescient work of Dr. Frankl, who foresaw the deep need for meaning in the modern world over seventy-five years ago.

Thank you to the Scribe tribe, especially Chas, Emily, Katie, Erik, AJ, Jess, Miles, Tara, and Tucker! I was consistently impressed by the quality of your support and guidance throughout this process.

A special thank you to my family, whose love and support I am grateful for.

About the Author

Jeff Smith, PhD, is a cognitive psychologist, inventor, and speaker who believes that compassion, persistence, and experimentation are the keys to solving any problem. Through live workshops, on-demand learning, and coaching, Jeff has empowered well over ten thousand people to deepen their skills in leadership, people management, giving and receiving feedback, deep listening, and learning.

Jeff, his partner, and their adorable, previously stray dogs are grateful to live among the Appalachian Mountains in the eastern USA.

Made in the USA
Columbia, SC
20 July 2022

63776770R00124